STEPS ALONG THE WAY

STEPS
ALONG
THE
WAY

A Governor's Scrapbook

Lamar Alexander

THOMAS NELSON PUBLISHERS
Nashville • Camden • New York

Photo by Howard H. Baker, Jr., 1968

For a thousand reasons,
This book is for Honey.

Published in Nashville, Tennessee, by Thomas Nelson,
Inc. and distributed in Canada by Lawson Falle, Ltd.,
Cambridge, Ontario.

Library of Congress Cataloging-in Publication Data

Alexander, Lamar.
  Steps along the way.

  1. Alexander, Lamar. 2. Tennessee—Governors—
Biography. 3. Tennessee—Politics and government—
1951-   . I. Title.
F440.3.A44A3   1986   976.8'053'0924 [B]   86-18184
ISBN 0-8407-4215-0

book designed by J. S. Laughbaum

Printed in the United States of America.

CONTENTS

FOREWORD

In the following pages Lamar Alexander hands us a kaleidoscopic view of the people, events, and circumstances he has experienced during his past eight years as the forty-fifth governor of Tennessee.

This volume—which Governor Alexander calls his "scrapbook" —is actually of much greater significance than that name might imply. Rather, the anecdotes herein reflect the inner character, personality, and basic nature of the man's steady succession of accomplishments. Time and again we see the governor's probing curiosity, his impulse to be creative, and his tendency to bypass the safe route and enter uncertain waters, if necessary, to seek and to achieve something he perceives to be worthwhile.

These anecdotes give insight into all these traits, reveal his omnipresent sense of humor and his very evident premier-class mind.

I believe no other governor has brought more international industry into his state. But Governor Alexander's greater accomplishment, I think, is that in an era that features cries of "protectionism" he has symbolized how international trading partners can cooperate to their mutual benefit. This must be the future direction of American industries and world industries if they are to expand and diversify and cooperate in order to survive.

Governor Alexander also has taken the concepts of home and family and local homefolks and generated them into "Tennessee Homecoming '86," which has pioneered the escalation of the spirit of a sovereign state. There is no way to measure the gift and the worth of the self-esteem that has permeated the state of Tennessee under this program.

It is not by any accident that this book also gives insights into the role played by Honey Alexander. Lamar Alexander is the very first to express how much her opinions and philosophies have contributed to his career.

As one who feels genuinely privileged to be counted a friend, I am glad that Lamar Alexander found the time to assemble and preserve this book's contents. The insights *Steps Along the Way* provides into his personality, spirit, and early formative influences are especially significant, because, in Governor Alexander, Tennessee has enjoyed a man who is among the greatest statesmen with which the Volunteer State has ever been blessed.

Alex Haley

People are always asking me: Do the murderers still serve meals at the Governor's Residence? Who thought of Tennessee Homecoming '86? Did a truck *really* hit you on your walk across the state? Who helps your kids with their homework? How did Saturn choose Tennessee? What kind of next door neighbor is Minnie Pearl?

This scrapbook answers these questions—and others—and tries to share with you what it's been like to be the governor of Tennessee for eight years. Answering the questions is not the only reason for the book. So many times I've wished others could laugh with me until their sides hurt rafting the Ocoee River with Jerry Reed, or stand by President Reagan while he comforts a widow at Fort Campbell, or eavesdrop on Marvin Runyon's telephone call telling me, "Nissan is coming to Tennessee!" or watch the second grader's eyes as she looked up into my face on her first visit to the Capitol and said, "I play the piano, too." Being governor has been too wonderful to bottle inside the memory of one person or even one family.

The best seat in the house is at the center of the stage, but occupying that seat has often been awkward for me. I have been tempted to watch the action when I am supposed to *be* the action. Almost every day I want to rush to tell someone what I have just heard or seen before I forget its specialness, to tell it with the urgency of a parent who repeats a child's first words to the parent who was not there. I feel that urgency especially because there is so much to share now: no stage in America is more interesting than Tennessee's. The nation has been admiring the way Tennessee communities are pioneering to improve our schools, roads, and jobs while putting on the biggest celebration in our history to boot! Tennessee is moving, and an unprecedented number of Tennesseans like the direction in which it is moving.

There is one caution: This scrapbook is full of private conversations, of stories and photographs most people haven't heard or seen before. But this is not a "hiss and tell" political book. I have never stood on the back of a pickup truck repeating private conversations of political allies—or rivals—in ways that would embarrass them, and I won't start now.

I am grateful to Marc Lavine, for her extensive help in collecting my "scraps." I have reimbursed the state for her time and for other expenses in connection with putting the scrapbook together. If I have seemed a little grumpy during the first half of this year, it was because I was waking up at 5:00 A.M., sometimes 4:00 A.M., to write the book. All the royalties go to our four children for their college education.

I hope my friends will understand that such a few pages leave out *most* of the people who worked the hardest to help me be governor. So this scrapbook—sharing my moments at the center of the stage—will be my way of saying thank you to those friends—and to *every* Tennessean—for giving me, twice, the very best job in the U.S.A. I hope they enjoy these memories as much as I've enjoyed the job.

Lamar Alexander

STEPS ALONG THE WAY

I t was a May evening in 1977.

"There is no need for Lamar to run again if he runs like he did in 1974. He has to be more natural, be himself." Honey was needlepointing furiously while telling campaign consultant Doug Bailey and me just what she thought about the 1978 governor's race. "Lamar can't spend all his time with the same Republican politicians the way he did before and the way Bill Brock did in 1976. He has to get out and meet the people, *walk* down the street where they live. Campaigning the way people campaign today really is dumb."

Honey doubted that I could win. Both Jake Butcher and Bob Clement looked strong for the Democratic nomination for governor in 1978 and both were way ahead of me in the early polls. Some reporters were even writing that it might be another half century before Tennessee had its next Republican governor. My defeat in the 1974 governor's race had interrupted my law practice, exhausted my savings, and disrupted our family. And there still was a twenty-five-thousand-dollar campaign debt.

"He could walk. Lamar could walk across the state," Doug Bailey said. Doug was from Washington, D.C., and he and his partner had helped to elect five of the twelve Republican governors still in office after Watergate and the Carter sweep.

"Walk and meet the people, play the trombone and the washboard like you did in New Orleans," Honey said.

"Shake a thousand hands a day," Doug continued. "Wear some clothes that everybody will recognize. Do what you like to do. That should be your campaign." I knew instantly they were right.

As bizarre as it sounds, walking across the state was the natural thing for me to do. I'd grown up walking in the Great Smoky Mountains, and I loved the outdoors. I hated political luncheons, cocktail parties, and formal dinners, none of which is needed on a six months' walk. There would also be no need to waste time flying from Memphis to Bristol and back to Nashville again in a small plane to meet with the same small groups of Republican leaders or to answer twenty telephone calls a day asking the inevitable campaign question that has no answer: "How's it going?"

It was so cold on the day we started the walk that one of the television camera batteries froze. My father was embarrassed, and my mother was sure I would be hit by a truck. I was.

I walked through the biggest snow-storms since 1938 from Butler to Mountain City at the eastern end of Tennessee. As I walked up Doe Valley, the local radio station took calls from people home from work and reported on my progress: "He's at Karl Pleasant's store. Ought to be at the church in about an hour." It was already February 23. I had been walking four weeks, and I was now ready to head west to Memphis, six hundred miles away.

Walkers don't need airplanes—except for going home on weekends— and the only available telephone would usually be in a booth beside the road.

I especially looked forward to getting out of coats and ties, which I don't like to wear. Honey liked a red and black Levi lumberjack shirt we found at a Murfreesboro store. I then bought every red and black shirt Harry Friedman had at his surplus store on Hillsboro Road in Nashville. I also bought about fifty pairs of socks and ten pairs of long underwear.

Spending the night along the way with seventy-five different families, people I had not known before, would put me back in touch with the kinds of homes and families I grew up with, the kind of people I'd lost touch with after going to Vanderbilt and New York University and working in big-city law firms. The entire experience would be a refresher course in what a governor needs to know.

And the walk would be great for television. "But it has to be real," Bailey insisted. "Television shows what is real and what is not. Fake a walk and everybody will know it."

So from Monday through Saturday, from January 26 to July 6, 1978, I walked 1,022 miles and lived with the people of Tennessee. Occasionally, I slipped away—most Saturday nights and once for our son Drew's championship hockey game. But every time I stopped I marked an X in the road with a piece of railroad chalk and came back to that X the next day to begin my walk.

Meeting people on *their* terms was like exploring. Even more fun

Traveling with Alexander's Wash-board Band became something like traveling with the Beatles. At Jellico High School, the students stood on their chairs and clapped their hands over their heads. When we finished playing, we escaped through the back door of the gym.

was Alexander's Washboard Band, four University of Tennessee band members, who walked along or drove a flatbed truck, and at the slightest suggestion hopped up on the truck bed with me and began to blare out "Mama don't 'low no washboard playing around here" on a combination of drums, electric piano, trombone, tuba, and washboard. It had been quite awhile since anyone had seen anything like this in Tennessee politics.

The walk started on my parents' front porch in Maryville. It was so cold that the trombone player's slide and the television camera battery froze. Because 40 percent of the state's voters live in East Tennessee and that was my political base, I walked east. On

Sometimes they let me do the play by play. During the winter of 1978, I saw three or four basketball games a week and usually was interviewed during the halftime about, say, the relative merits of the Mosheim and the MacDonald elementary school teams.

13

I shook one thousand hands a day and waved at every car or truck I passed. By the time I reached Middle Tennessee, some people were beginning to wave back, and there were smiles of recognition on their faces. Whenever I stopped walking for the day, I put an X down and went back to it when I started again.

February 23, I reached Mountain City at the eastern tip of the state.

In Mountain City, I was closer to Canada than I was to Memphis. The governorship seemed a long way away. I had trudged through two feet of snow, the biggest snowfall—so they told me in Butler—since 1938. As I walked up Doe Valley most people were home from work, watching out their windows, listening to the local radio station report telephone calls from people who had seen me: "He's walking up by Karl Pleasant's store and ought to be at the Baptist Church in another hour."

Each March day the grass grew greener. The weather was not cold enough anymore for long underwear. A few fishermen began to recognize my red and black shirt as they drove by. One woman in Carter's Valley hollered at the Washboard Band and me as we walked past her farm: "Hey, you boys quit shooting my rabbits! Get on out of here and quit shooting my rabbits." A half hour later I finally convinced her that she ought to vote for me for governor instead of running me off.

The next day, Joe Simmons stopped me along the side of Highway 11–W and drove me to his farm in Stanley Valley for peanut butter sandwiches. He told me how his father had driven him in a wagon to the Hawkins County Courthouse in 1920 to hear Alf Taylor tell stories about his coon dog "Limber," the last time an East Tennessean had been elected governor.

Imagine what a politician can do and say while shaking one thousand hands a day for seven days in Hawkins or Greene counties. You can meet almost everyone who might vote in the Republican Primary, dominate the front page of the newspaper, *every day,* learn what people think about the property tax rate, whether the state officials really need a Lear jet, how much teachers spend from their own pockets on textbooks for their students, whether the duck season needs to be longer, whether the local nursing home really is in good shape, or whether Highway 11–W needs to be finished. After spending nights with families and eating their green beans and roasting ears and country ham and hearing their prayers, it is very hard *not* to be in touch with the people of Tennessee or not to feel very confident about knowing what their needs really are.

I quickly learned that the most important source of news is neighbor talking to neighbor. Second comes the local radio news, usually heard at 6:00 A.M. There is not much talk about the great Washington issues, which are usually debated on television in Washington language. There *is* a lot of talk about—whether the local school is good, whether the road in front of the house is paved, whether the plant where people work will shut down, whether the garbage truck will be on time, and whether it is safe to go out at night. The voters are smarter than the politicians. One Hawkins County lady told me, ''I'll tell you how to get elected.'' I listened carefully since I had six hundred miles to go to Memphis. ''Don't make any promises—we've heard them all before. Just do the best you can. Second, keep the taxes down; we can't afford more. Third, for heaven's sake, behave yourself when you get in! We're sick and tired of being embarrassed by all those politicians we hear about on the radio.''

First reactions to the walk were, at best, skeptical. Most Capitol Hill reporters who attended the start of the walk from my parents' front porch in Maryville rode around in warm cars writing stories about how I had just thrown away whatever chance I'd ever had to be elected governor. The first truck driver whose hand I tried to shake rolled up his window. One of my Upper East Tennessee campaign managers refused to meet me at the county line because he was embarrassed to be seen with a character who would walk through the winter rain wearing a red and black shirt. And a number of big Republicans in Nashville were ready to disown me.

What bothered them most was how I ''looked.'' The last straw was when I appeared on the first statewide television debate. The other eleven candidates wore coats and ties; I wore my red and black shirt. "Get that shirt off him!" some of the big fundraisers and politicians shouted at Tom Ingram, my campaign manager. "He's lost his mind and he's going to lose the election." What they didn't understand was that I was happy and comfortable walking along, shaking hands, wearing a red and black shirt, and saying to at least one thousand people a day, "Hello, I'm Lamar Alexander and I'd like to be your next governor." Being happy and comfortable—and being yourself—is probably the most important thing for a candidate to do. And what the Nashville politicians had forgotten was that to most people in Tennessee I didn't look funny at all. Most Tennesseans don't wear suits and ties to work.

Still, my father was a little embarrassed by the whole adventure, and my mother was sure that I would be hit by a truck. She was right. In Newport, on only the ninth day of my walk, a white pickup flipped me over its hood. "Oh my God," said the driver as she leaped from the truck and saw who was lying in the main street with campaign brochures scattered all over. "Why did it have to happen in Newport?"

Newport merchants who had heard the truck brakes squeal pressed their noses almost through their front store windows and

'YOU GET GREAT IDEAS, LAMAR— BUT I THINK YOU NEED TO WORK ON YOUR TIMING'

16

watched, wide-eyed. My left foot stung, but I got up quickly, embarrassed. I gathered the brochures as fast as I could and limped on across the street into Overholt's hardware store and, as if nothing had happened, began passing out brochures to people who still were reluctant to unstick their noses from the store windowpanes.

Then I limped to the town infirmary. For the next thirty minutes a doctor x-rayed and examined my ankle, which was already beginning to swell. Without my heavy boots, it surely would have been broken. Meanwhile, the Washboard Band, with son Drew experimenting on the drums, was entertaining a crowd by the Cocke County Courthouse. No one had missed me. I rushed to join them, carefully watching for white pickup trucks and favoring my tender left foot, which was tightly wrapped inside a loosely tied boot. After lunch with the county political leaders, I drove to our cabin in Miller's Cove. For the first time I noticed the splash of white paint on the left shoulder of my red jacket where the truck hit. I rested and healed for three days, missing part of Morristown. I faithfully made up that omission two weekends later.

The sun grew warmer, and so did my reception as I climbed from Spring City to Grassy Cove on the Cumberland Plateau. I had been on the road for fifteen weeks, always walking along the left side of the road, avoiding my natural enemies—lightning, dogs, and trucks—and waving at every passing car. Some motorists were beginning to smile, to wave back, and even to honk. When I shook hands, more faces lit up in recognition. Television coverage of the walk was helping. To have some on-the-spot coverage of my walk in DeKalb County, a Nashville TV reporter asked if he could film a conversation between me and a man named Luke, who did odd jobs for Representative Frank Buck. So, for the benefit of the camera, I said to Luke, "I'm Lamar Alexander and I'd like to be your next governor."

"I think we can work something out," said Luke. "For two dollars I'll vote for you and I'll get all the people around here to vote for you just like I do it for Frank." Middle Tennesseans saw the conversation on Channel 5 that night.

Robin Robertson and Reggie Reeves, students at Middle Tennessee State University, met me at the Rutherford-Cannon County line and walked along for three days. At Lascassas Elementary School, we waved at children whose teachers had let them perch, like a long row of jaybirds, on a fence by the road. In Murfreesboro I found Dr. Henry King Butler, a college classmate, who cut sore corns off my small toes. My supply of red and black shirts diminished and replacements were harder to find. Supporters began to sell my autographed red and black shirts to raise campaign money. At an auction at a Columbia rally, someone paid $500. My stock was going up.

Ross Blakely, age twelve, had written inviting me to stay with his family when I walked through McNairy County. I arrived at their home in Eastview just in time for supper June 14. Then, since it was Wednesday night, we all went to the Ramer Baptist Church.

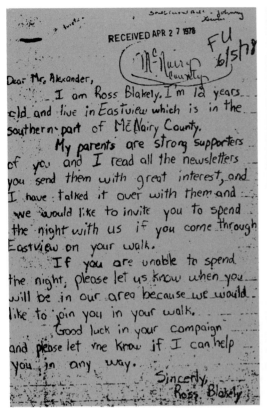

RECEIVED APR 2 7 1978

Dear Mr. Alexander,

    I am Ross Blakely. I'm 1[?] years old and live in Eastview which is in the southern part of McNairy County.

    My parents are strong supporters of you and I read all the newsletters you send them with great interest, and I have talked it over with them and we would like to invite you to spend the night with us if you come through Eastview on your walk.

    If you are unable to spend the night, please let us know when you will be in our area because we would like to join you in your walk.

    Good luck in your campaign and please let me know if I can help you in any way.

             Sincerely,
             Ross Blakely

It's hard for me to imagine how much the Blakely family—and all seventy-five families I stayed with—have changed in just eight years. I saw both Ross and Lora Lee, who was a cute fifth grader in 1978, when they attended Boys and Girls State. Ross will be a senior in accounting next year at Memphis State, and Lora Lee will enter Union University. Jeremy, who in 1978 could walk just well enough to dance with the Washboard Band, is now a third grader. Johnny, the dad, still works with South Central Bell and has been elected to the school board. When Jeremy started school, Linda, the mom, went to work and is now the executive secretary of the McNairy County Chamber of Commerce.

After that, I visited with neighbors in the Blakely living room until 10:00 P.M. I was ready for bed.

The next morning I got up at 5:30 A.M. to visit the Levi factory in Ramer. The women coming to work at six complimented my shirt. When I went inside I realized why. They were making them. Most of Levi's red and black shirts of the kind I wore were being made right there in Ramer, Tennessee.

I knew I was being taken more seriously when Charles Crawford, a Memphis State University history professor, walked along with me through Fayette County in the hot June sun to make an oral history tape. Then, when Honey and the children met me on July 6 in the one-hundred-degree heat in Memphis along with five hundred supporters and families with whom I had stayed from all over Tennessee, I knew more than ever the walk had been the right thing to do. We walked down Beale Street and stuck our feet into the Mississippi River mud. I felt great. The walk had helped my campaign. But, most important, it would make me a better governor if I was lucky enough to win.

It was July 6 and one hundred degrees when we walked down Beale Street in Memphis. Honey and the children joined me (Will was not yet born), as well as five hundred friends from all over Tennessee, many of them families I had spent the night with. We stuck our feet into the Mississippi River mud together.

THREE DAYS EARLY

When I woke up early that Wednesday, Honey was already busy in the living room, shoving around packed boxes. Our home in the Green Hills area of Nashville looked like a tornado had blown through each room. There were clothes in boxes and dishes in crates, furniture stacked in the middle of the room, and rugs rolled up by the wall. Toys filled other boxes. One pile of things would go to our mountain cabin in East Tennessee. The rest we would move today to the mansion on South Curtiswood Lane. In three days I would be governor of Tennessee.

At least that was the "official plan." A cloud, dark as those outside in the winter sky, cast a shadow on one of the happiest weeks of my life. My predecessor, Governor Ray Blanton, was in hot water for his clemency actions, and people from both sides of the political stream had begun to insist that I take office early, which would be an unprecedented action.

Honey would like to forget that day, January 17, 1979, but she can't. She remembers it the way everybody else does: the rain, the icy mush, the thirty-five-degree weather that is standard for an inaugural week. It was "cold, gray, and horrible."

To her the whole idea of my taking office early was "just plain stupid." "Why let Ray Blanton ruin two inaugurations in a row?" she asked. "He beat you in 1974. That ruined one. And, if you take office early because of the way he is acting now, he'll ruin another one."

The Blantons, in fact, had tried to be helpful during the transition and had offered to move out of the Governor's Residence a few days early so we could move in before thousands of inaugural visitors descended upon Nashville—and us. A few weeks earlier Governor Blanton's wife, Betty, had taken Honey on a tour of the Residence, showing her where the childrens' rooms could be, but Mrs. Blanton did not show Honey the master bedroom. The governor and his advisors were having a meeting in there. His legal counsel, accused of selling clemencies, had been arrested that day. During *my* visit a few days later, Governor Blanton did show me the bedroom. "I got a new bed when Dunn left," he said. "I wouldn't sleep on the same bed Dunn slept on."

21

Honey packed and shoved boxes while the state troopers and sheriff's deputies from Williamson County—specially assigned to guard us—moved respectfully from room to room. When we had arrived home on election night two months earlier, the deputies had been waiting for us. "They couldn't be nicer," Honey often said, "but it's always hard to have strangers in your home." They were there when we got up, when we ate in the kitchen, when we went to bed, even when we argued. They slept in the den and did their best to stay out of the way.

Drew was nine then. He tossed a ball on the front porch, waiting for his ride to school. Leslee, who was six, was staying home from school because of her cough. Dressed in her nightgown and bathrobe, she moved from mattress to mattress on the upstairs bedroom floors as the packing progressed. Kathryn, only four, stayed as near to Honey as possible. Everything that was important to her was being packed and pushed and taken away.

We had realized after the election that we would probably never know again the comfortable quiet of our Green Hills home. But moving day made us painfully aware that we were not just losing our privacy but our home as well. "Moving days are never very pleasant," Honey reminded me as I escaped into the cold rain, heading to my hideaway office only a few blocks away on Hobbs Road to work on Saturday's inaugural address—the most important speech of my life. I had no public appearances scheduled. The last of the preinaugural receptions (we had already shaken hands with fifteen thousand Tennesseans at five preinaugural receptions) would be in Jackson tonight. I was dressed the way I like to dress, casually: "Unpresentable," Honey assured me as I got into the trooper's car, "for anything but the back yard."

A little before noon Hal Hardin, the U.S. Attorney, interrupted my speech writing at the office. His telephone call wasted no words: "Governor Blanton is about to release some state prisoners who we believe have bought their way out of prison. Will you take office, as soon as you can, to stop him?" Hardin's call stunned me. I asked him to give the same information to the Lt. Governor and the Speaker of the House. I wanted to think about the consequences of such an unprecedented action. I called Honey. Then I called Hardin back just after noon. I did not want my ears to play tricks on me. Too much was at stake. I asked him to tell me again exactly what he had told me in the first call. He repeated his message and told me he had talked with Attorney General William Leech who would talk with the Speakers. It was like having an elephant put in my front yard. I could not ignore the call from a respected Democratic U.S. Attorney whom Blanton himself had once appointed judge. So I began to plan—with other state officials—a conspiracy to deprive Tennessee's sitting governor of his office three days early.

As he drove me home for lunch Herchel Winstead, the state trooper, said: "You'll be governor by tonight." I was afraid he was right.

I ate quickly. Our home suddenly seemed so lonely and empty. When I left again for the office, Honey was sitting on a stool in the bare kitchen drinking coffee and serving chicken salad sandwiches to impatient children who watched while strange men carried the last of their toys, clothes, and beds to a big, fenced house on the other side of town. I called her two or three times that afternoon in between conversations with the Speakers and the attorney general. I described to her the secret coup we were engineering.

Honey wondered if everything we had planned for Saturday would come to nothing. What about the high school bands that had practiced for weeks to march in the parade? What about the thousands of people who had made reservations? Why couldn't I make a decision? This talk about an early swearing in had gone on and on and on.

I thought about how tired she must be—the campaign, the children, the bouncing airplane rides as we flew home from receptions on stormy nights, the move, and now the absurdity of sitting in an empty house wondering whether I would be governor in three hours or three days.

"And what about clothes?" she asked when I called the last time, at 3:00 P.M. "The clothes are all on the moving van. How can you be sworn in?"

Going home again at 4:30 was like saying an unexpected second good-by to an old friend. To complicate things, Leslee's cough was worse, Kathryn still clung to Honey the way a baby koala bear hangs on its mother, and Drew announced that he would not go with us to the Supreme Court Building where I would be sworn in as governor.

I tried to help Drew understand what had happened. He had spent some time on my campaign walk. He knew of Governor Blanton's problems and that Saturday would be a very important day. But this was *Wednesday*. Why did I have to be sworn in three days early, without telling anybody, and while we were moving?

Clothes arrived from all over town. I borrowed a belt and red tie from Tom Ingram. State troopers fished a blue suit out of a box of my clothes already at the Governor's Residence. Honey found a blue dress in her closet (it had been "absolutely forgotten") and a pair of shoes. A friend brought her some stockings. Leslee borrowed a dress from Sara Hardison, who lived a block away. Drew and Kathryn looked "shabby" in their school clothes, Honey thought, but "there is nothing I can do about that."

Near dark, at 5:20 P.M., we left our home for the last time. Drew had finally agreed to go with us. Honey carried Leslee, who began to cough even more in the cold air. I had helped Kathryn put on her little boots, and for a change she clung to me, the only available parent. We crowded—the five of us and Tom Ingram and Herchel Winstead—into one unmarked patrol car and headed downtown.

The children jabbered. The adults were quiet. At 5:40 we pulled into the basement parking garage at the back of the Supreme Court

Building just across Seventh Avenue from the Capitol. Bill Koch, still working then for Attorney General Leech, met us. We moved quickly to the elevator. For the first time I noticed that Honey was carrying the big family Bible, the one that my great-grandparents Alexander had used when they married in Blount County in 1868. "I had saved it back," she explained. "I know how things get lost in moves and I knew you would want it on Saturday. The Bible was one thing I was going to move myself because I know how important it is to you."

As I stepped from the elevator on the first floor I sensed for the first time the electricity of the moment: reporters, staff members, and some friends were pushing into the Supreme Court room from every direction.

None of them had known about the ceremony until forty minutes earlier. Tom Ingram had told the staff at 5:00 P.M. to come to the Supreme Court Building in thirty minutes, but he had not told them why. He also had called former Watergate counsel Fred Thompson home from Washington to help sort out the pardons scandal, but did not tell Fred why he needed to come within a few hours.

Rumors of every sort had spread through the Capitol, including one that Governor Blanton was about to release James Earl Ray, the convicted murderer of Martin Luther King. Most of those crowding into the courtroom had no idea what they were rushing to see.

The ceremony began at 5:56 P.M. Honey held the Bible, opened to my father's favorite verse, II Timothy 2:15: "Study to show thyself approved unto God, a workman that needeth not to be ashamed, rightly dividing the word of truth."

Leslee and Kathryn put their hands on the Bible when I put mine there. Still coughing, Leslee flipped through the pages of the Bible while I took the oath. Drew looked straight ahead into stunned faces. The Democratic state officials stood behind me, grim as pallbearers at a good friend's funeral.

The ceremony ended six minutes later. The crowd, filled with relief, burst into cheers. The reporters surged forward, climbing over the courtroom railings, standing on the polished cherry tables. To help, Honey held their microphones with both hands. Tears streamed down her cheeks. "I've just had a cold," she explained.

After twenty minutes of questions we fought our way to the judges' chambers. A cameraman almost pushed Honey down. As we left I lifted Kathryn. The toes of her boots were pointed in the wrong directions. I had put them on the wrong feet. I made them right. The family left for the Governor's Residence. I grabbed a hamburger and milkshake and slept in the back seat while troopers drove a state patrol car to Jackson in fog and rain. We arrived two hours late for what was to have been the last preinaugural reception. Five thousand people were still waiting for what turned out to be the first event for a new governor.

It was 1:30 A.M. before I arrived back in Nashville for my first night at the Governor's Residence. Honey woke up. We were both so tired we had nothing left to say. It took us two minutes to go to sleep on the mattress that Governor Blanton had used for four years, minus three days.

My Scribbled Notes from the Wastebasket the Afternoon of the Early Swearing In. From noon to 3:30 I had wrestled with whether to take office three days early. It seemed like something that might happen in Latin America, but not in the United States. Lieutenant Governor Wilder had said it was unconstitutional. One thing was sure: I wouldn't do it unless the Democratic Speakers of the Senate and House and the attorney general agreed. These notes (see illustration) are the statement we worked out after a dozen phone calls between my hideaway office and the Capitol, where they were meeting. The notes also reflect what else I worried about. Who would tell Governor Blanton he had been replaced? (Attorney General William Leech did five minutes before I became governor. But Blanton had just heard it from CBS News.)

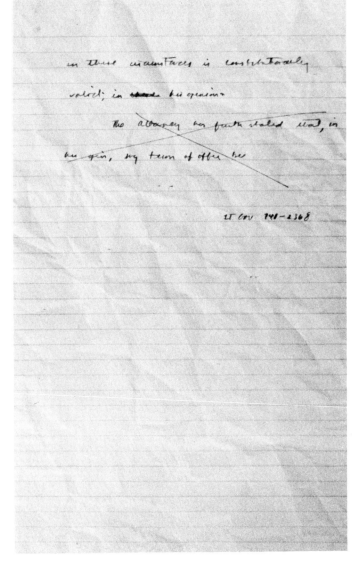

Additional security for Blanton? (Yes.) Would Blanton attend Saturday's second inauguration? (He publicly declined before we had to decide.) I also seriously considered other things that today seem unthinkable: *What if Blanton calls up the National Guard or orders the highway patrol to defend the Capitol? What if two governors show up for work, at the same job, in the same office, at the same time, each with an army in tow?*

I told Tom Ingram, when we were discussing our options, "This is the kind of thing where fifty things can go wrong and forty-nine of them probably will." We did it anyway. After I left my office to take the family to the early swearing in, Tom picked these crumpled notes out of the wastebasket.

Drawing by Sandy Campbell
Courtesy of the *Tennessean*

Securing the Capitol. As soon as I was sworn in I asked Tom Ingram and Lewis Donelson to secure the Capitol, to keep things as they were, to be as polite as possible.

Donelson went to the basement of the Capitol building to the office of Robert Lillard, Blanton's legal counsel. On Lillard's desk were stacks of documents—clemencies and pardons ready for Blanton's review.

Lillard, about six feet six inches tall, confronted Donelson, about a foot shorter.

Donelson told Lillard that he could not take anything out of his office.

Lillard called Blanton on the telephone, and Donelson told Blanton the same thing.

"You mean I'm not allowed to come to the Capitol to get my papers?" asked Blanton.

"That's right," said Donelson.

"By whose authority?" demanded Blanton.

"By the governor's authority," said Donelson.

"I am the governor!" said Blanton.

"Not anymore," said Donelson.

"Four Stormy Years Ended in an Evening's Gentle Rain"—so wrote the Associated Press reporter who was among those who met Governor Blanton at his home about 7:30 that evening.

"How do you feel?"

"Saddened," said Blanton. "Saddened for the people of Tennessee because of this terrible and embarrassing action."

"How did you find out about it?"

"I heard about it on television. There is such a thing as courtesy. I thought they would have the courtesy to tell me."

"Have you talked with the new governor?"

"The new governor informed me through Lewis Donelson that I'm not allowed to get the desk and the chair that I had in Congress, and I'm not allowed to get my papers out. The new governor has secured the Capitol building. I didn't know a governor could do that."

How My Parents Found Out

Mother and Dad had left home around ten after six (Eastern Standard Time) for the annual congregational meeting at New Providence Presbyterian Church in Maryville. The meeting began at 6:30 P.M. with a covered dish dinner. After eating, Mother began doing her share of washing dishes in the kitchen.

At about ten after seven Hugh Crawford, Jr., came up to her and said, "Flo, the radio says that Lamar was just sworn in as governor."

Mother replied, "Hugh, he wouldn't do anything like that without telling us."

The congregational meeting began. Part way through it, a friend passed a note all the way across the room to Mother. "Lamar has been sworn in as governor in Nashville."

Mother didn't show the note to Dad until after the meeting was over. They drove home, arriving about 8:05 and called my campaign office in Nashville. It was 7:05 there, more than an hour after the swearing in. I was on my way to Jackson.

"Mrs. Alexander, we've been trying to reach you for forty-five minutes," an aide said. "Lamar tried to call you earlier. He's the governor now. He wanted you to know."

Inaugurations Are the Difference between Us and a Banana Republic or the Soviet Union, I kept thinking as I looked at a plaza full of colorful umbrellas in the freezing rain. In 1969 I had watched Lyndon Johnson hand over the most power in the world to a man he disliked, Richard Nixon, all in a simple, civil ceremony. In America the torch is always passed peacefully and with grace.

Rain on the inaugural parade. I'm walking in it in my red and black shirt.

When an elected official raises his right hand, traffic stops, attention turns, and emotions run high. (Dan Rather—who is as hard-bitten as any reporter—cried on the air, in front of millions of Americans, simply trying to say that America was the land of the free and the home of the brave during President Reagan's inauguration in 1985.) So this second inauguration as governor of Tennessee within three days was more than legal insurance for the earlier hurry-up swearing in. It was the only way for citizens to validate their free election. An inauguration is a peculiarly American rite of passage. It is more for the people than for their elected official.

Honey and I danced on Saturday night at each of the three inaugural balls, barely finding room to move. No one seemed to mind the crush. Honey was obviously pregnant with our fourth child. (She had not told me she was pregnant until after the November election.) Her gown will end up at the State Museum where it will be, I suppose, the only inaugural maternity gown.

It was beginning to snow when we crawled into bed early Sunday morning. By daybreak six inches of snow lay on the ground. Honey loves to remember how happy she awakened to the blanket of white. "It was clean, sweet snow. Everything was washed clean again. It was so white, pretty, and sparkling."

The icy streets and predictions of an overflowing crowd—and perhaps the late Saturday night inaugural parties—left many empty seats at Nashville's Westminster Presbyterian Church at the special inaugural worship service on Sunday morning, January 21. My sister Jane's husband, the Reverend William J. Carl, III, preached the inaugural sermon, ". . . So Help Me, God." Senator Howard Baker was so impressed that, when he returned to Washington, he put Bill's sermon in the *Congressional Record.* Since then I have read it many times. Here are some excerpts from the sermon:

And what did Solomon pray for? "Give therefore thy servant an understanding heart to govern thy people, that I may discern between good and evil." What does he call himself? A servant. "Give thy servant." Solomon recognized that even as a king he was a servant—a servant of God and a servant of the people. Any leader who forgets that forfeits his right to lead. And what did he desire? An understanding heart—and here the Hebrew means almost literally a "hearing" heart—a receptive mind, one that listens and considers before it decides, one that can hear the voice of God and the voice of the people. But Solomon also prays for the ability to discern between good and evil. How difficult that is to do even today; for in real life distinction between good and evil is never as clear cut as the good guys and the bad guys or the characters in *Star Wars.*

Every area of our lives, whether in politics, business, or the church, is fraught with compromise and gray-area decisions. Decisions about who to trust or who to believe in government are laden with ambiguity. As one of my colleagues at Union Seminary, John Leith, has said, ". . . we ought never to underestimate the residual powers of goodness in evil people nor should we ever underestimate the power of evil in good people. . . . The good are never as good as they think they are and the bad are never as bad as they are thought to be." This is still true today, even in government.

The prayer then for the ability to discern between good and evil should not be taken lightly. What Solomon prayed for essentially was that he be a good man—something all public officials should covet. Lamar's mother told me not long ago that all she has ever prayed for Lamar since he was a child was that he be a good man. . . .

We live in a time when hardly anything lasts. Our money seems gone before we get it. Our children are grown-up and gone before we know them. Our spouses die and leave us alone. To the tick-tock of our rockers we play "Only Yesterday." Sooner or later, we all realize that hardly anything lasts, not nations, not even us. To trust only in each other is a fatal mistake. History books are littered with examples of leaders who trusted only in their own power and ability, and both they and their people suffered for it. But who needs to read history when it happens in our time? Leaders ousted from office or taken out before their term has expired. It's the mark of our decade. . . .

Trusting in the Lord should never be done with unreasonable expectations. I think Lamar understands that. Trust in the Lord never means instant miracles, instant solutions to all public problems. We pray not for instant solutions but for the wisdom and understanding to do what is right. . . .

The events of the inaugural week closed with a reception for the public Sunday afternoon at the Residence. Between 1:00 and 5:00 P.M. we counted five thousand visitors. We shook hands at the rate of about twenty per minute for four hours. Many of the visitors stood outside in the cold and snow for an hour and a half. Honey decided then and there to open the Residence on a regular basis to the public.

POLITICS: WINNING AND LOSING

Flying over Memphis at night in 1966, seeing those thousands of lights running to the Mississippi River, I wondered, *Could Howard Baker ever really be Senator of all that?*

Just the *idea* of campaigning for a statewide office was revolutionary for Tennessee Republicans. Before 1966, Tennessee had never elected a Republican senator. *Never.* Carroll Reece had tried in 1948 and had even persuaded Roy Acuff to run on the same ticket for governor. But at the rallies the crowds would drift away when Acuff stopped singing and Reece started speaking. In the election Acuff got more votes for governor against Gordon Browning than Reece did against Estes Kefauver. The election of the last Republican governor in 1920 had so disturbed the Democratic legislature that it had repealed most of the governor's powers for two years until another Democratic governor could be safely installed.

I joined Howard Baker's campaign in July of 1966 for three hundred dollars a month. I was in between a law clerkship and joining a Knoxville firm; I thought Tennessee needed a two-party system; and I liked what I knew of Baker, whose father had been our congressman. I couldn't have picked a teacher with better instincts, and I quickly learned some of the basics of campaigning:

- Press releases are sometimes as good as press conferences.
- Television reporters have 3:30 P.M. deadlines, earlier than the newspaper people.
- It's better not to shout into a television camera.
- Television may introduce you to people in a way that newspapers can't, but newspapers set the political agenda in a way that television never can.
- Be on time. At least you will look like you know what you're doing.
- Don't do anything that you don't want to read about on the front page of tomorrow's newspaper.

As the Baker bandwagon rolled across Tennessee, I discovered some other political truths I never would have imagined:

31

- Most East Tennessee political leaders still bear their great-grand-fathers' grudges, so it is often better simply to buy a lot of radio ads rather than to be seen by the leader of one faction with the leader of another.
- There are more Democrats than Republicans in Tennessee, but, fortunately, they bear old grudges just as well as Republicans; and since there are more Democrats, there are more Democratic grudges.
- Baker's Republican appeal to black voters did more than attract black support. The appeal was just as important to white voters who agreed that Republicans should make such appeals...and to white voters who thought that Republicans should not.
- Political big shots can defeat you, but they can't elect you.

Then I learned the most crucial fundamental: getting the talk right. The "talk" can be generally defined as the answer to the classic campaign question, "How's it going?" which is what one important politician always asks another important politician. In the 1966 Baker campaign, overcoming the notion that a Republican could never win a statewide race was our biggest early obstacle. It was the job of the campaign manager, John B. Waters, Jr., to travel back and forth between East and West Tennessee telling political leaders how good everything was in the *other* end of the state. He did this for approximately the same reason that a UT cheerleader runs from one end of Shields-Watkins field to the other on Saturday afternoons in October to build momentum for the Volunteers.

Watching Howard Baker taught me that politics requires all the gall a person can muster. Imagine yourself standing alone on the Grainger County Courthouse steps bellowing to about thirty-five people. Some of the men are chewing and spitting, some are swapping knives, most are gossiping with each other, almost no one is watching the speaker. But all of them expect you to keep bellowing—if you are to be considered a serious candidate. It's a ritual in Tennessee politics, and it's not for the ordinary, modest man or woman. Howard Baker's generous personal serving of gall showed through in 1964 when he passed up his father's safe congressional seat to make his first run for the U.S. Senate, a decision his father's friends thought approached lunacy. As it turned out, he might have won if Barry Goldwater had not offered to sell the TVA while standing on the same campaign platform with Howard at the Knoxville Airport. Running again in 1966 was bold enough, but predicting a week before the election that he would win by one hundred thousand votes struck me then as gall-gone-crazy. "Do you really think you can win by one hundred thousand votes?" I asked him. "I do," he answered. And when he did, I started paying more attention to his political instincts.

Howard Baker has the brains, judgment, and extra-dimension personality that make him my favorite candidate for president. Some people in public life may arrive better prepared, but no one rises to the occasion as well as Howard Baker. And he has always had a gift for being partisan and ambitious without seeming to be either.

My apprenticeship with Howard has blossomed into friendship, one that is about as close as two people can have in political life. Our friendship has not continued because we spend much time together or because we always agree—we don't. I avoided his 1972 campaign to have more time with my family, and I declined his offer to be the Republican counsel for the Watergate Committee. I did not want to go back to Washington, and I did not have the stomach for investigating people with whom I had worked. And he was disappointed in 1982 and 1984 when I did not run to join him or to succeed him in the U.S. Senate.

But I've tried to help Howard whenever I felt he really needed it, and I always will. When he was elected Republican leader of the U.S. Senate in 1977, I returned to Washington for three months to help organize his staff. It has worked both ways. I cannot remember a time when he did not leave a meeting to take a call from me while I was governor and he was Majority Leader. As a result, the Ocoee River is opened to rafters, the Distinguished Scientists Program is flourishing at Oak Ridge and UT–Knoxville, and the Anderson-Tully Basin is purchased with federal money—and on and on and on . . .

Our friendship has survived where most politicians' friendships fail—even in the tension of running together on the same ticket. Perhaps it is because of mutual respect, perhaps because we don't expect too much of each other. Maybe it's the little things. When Honey and I returned from our honeymoon, Howard and his wife, Joy, were at our house with flowers. When I walked across the state, Joy sent me a glass turtle. My father's birthday and Howard's were on the same day, November 15, and Howard rarely forgot. And I know of no one, outside my family, more genuinely interested in what I might do with the rest of my life than Howard Baker.

Hiring "Red 'n' Fred" for the First District Tour Was My First Big Political Job. The conventional wisdom in 1966 was that a Republican candidate had to show off Congressman Jimmy Quillen's support on the Saturday before the general election with a tour of Quillen's district. The Quillen-Baker (not Baker-Quillen) bandwagon began at 9:00 A.M. Pickin' and singin' by Red 'n Fred, from grocer Cas Walker's early morning Knoxville television show, drew the crowd close to the steps of the Sevier County Courthouse. The local Republican chairman introduced Congressman Quillen while Red 'n Fred rushed ahead to the Dandridge Courthouse steps to begin drawing the next crowd. Quillen stirred the electorate in Sevierville—he even claimed credit for the sun coming out as it pushed aside the morning mist—and finally introduced Baker. The voters crowded close to hear Baker's surprisingly big voice, and stayed around after the politicians' bus had left, arguing about whether the Democrats would get as many as one thousand votes in the county on election day or any votes at all on Locust Ridge.

Saturday morning courthouse crowds were still big in 1966; people wanted to touch their politicians when hearing their politics. And that encouraged the politicians. By the late afternoon stop in Rogersville, the storytelling was nearly as good as that of the campaigns one hundred years ago when the candidates came only once, spoke for three hours, and rode on confidently—knowing there would be no one in the next county who could contradict anything that had been said in the last county.

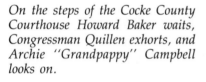

On the steps of the Cocke County Courthouse Howard Baker waits, Congressman Quillen exhorts, and Archie "Grandpappy" Campbell looks on.

In this photograph I guess Bill and I were enjoying thinking about which Democrat to pound with the auctioneer's gavel. The map behind us shows the route (and an alternate route) of my walk across the state. It has hung behind my desk in my office at the Capitol the eight years I've been governor.

"The *U.S.* Senate?" That was the incredulous reaction of Mae Ross McDowell, age seventy-one, former mayor of Johnson City, when I, at age twenty-nine, asked what she thought of my running for the U.S. Senate in the 1970 Republican Primary against Bill Brock. Mrs. McDowell's reaction was one of the more favorable reactions I received from about two dozen Tennessee Republican leaders when I asked them the same question during a three-day trip across Tennessee during January of 1970. My former roommates in Washington had talked me into taking the trip as a last-ditch effort to bring me to my senses. I agreed to make the trip if one of them, Lee Smith, would go with me.

My last visit was in Memphis with a Republican dentist who was thinking about running for governor, which seemed to me the only political idea that was more ridiculous than my running for the Senate. The dentist, Winfield Dunn, in a wonderfully inoffensive way also told me I shouldn't run. Now I'm glad I didn't. Bill Brock won the election, later became the best Republican National Chairman in the country's history, and is a good friend. He has been the block builder of the Tennessee Republican party.

I Wanted to Make the Most of My Five Minutes. I had worked for a year and a half in a small cubicle, forty feet from the Oval Office, taking phone messages for the president's aide, Bryce Harlow. In August of 1970, I was going home to manage Winfield Dunn's general election campaign for governor.

"Good luck," the president said. "Tennessee and Indiana are the two states with the meanest politics I know." (Rather than "meanest," Mr. Nixon used a colorful agricultural term describing what cattlemen do to young bulls to turn them into steers.)

My visit was a "stand up." Oval Office visitors who were allowed to "sit down" tended to get comfortable and stay a while. It usually meant the difference between five minutes and fifteen minutes of the president's time.

I left Washington having learned a lot from watching Mr. Harlow, but I had rarely seen the president.

"Have You Told It All, Winfield? Have You Told It All?" John Jay Hooker thought he had Winfield Dunn right where he wanted him. It was late in the 1970 campaign. Reporters from the Nashville *Tennessean* had uncovered a story about Winfield's slugging a man in Mississippi and getting arrested. Without revealing the story, Hooker began to say at every campaign stop, "Have you told it all, Winfield? Have you told it all?" We tried to shield Dunn from reporters, but finally Jerry Thompson of the *Tennessean* asked the question and the story came out. It turned out that in the sixties, Winfield had punched a man who had insulted Winfield's wife, Betty.

After the story ran, Bill Jenkins, the former Republican Speaker of the House, called me in Nashville. I could feel his excitement all the way to the other end of the telephone line in East Tennessee. "That story's worth a hundred thousand votes up here. A man *ought* to defend his wife. Why didn't you boys bring that out sooner?"

Dunn spent eighty thousand dollars in his primary, had no debt when he finished, and as late as Labor Day, had no campaign manager, no professional pollster, and no general election finance chairman or advertising agency. He became the first Republican governor since Alf Taylor was elected in the Warren G. Harding sweep in 1920.

"Sometimes You're Up, Sometimes You're Down, and You're Not Always Up" (a famous political saying by J. Hugh Branson). Tennessee Republicans were up in September 1974 when we held both U.S. Senate seats, the governorship, and five of eight congressional seats. And for a general election opponent, I had just drawn Ray Blanton, who had won only 23 percent of the Democratic Primary vote. Things looked so rosy I took the family to Palm

Robin Beard, Dortch Oldham, Howard Baker, Winfield Dunn, Jane Hardaway, Bill Brock, Lamar Alexander, John Duncan, Dan Kuykendall, La Mar Baker, Jimmy Quillen, and Nat Winston, September 1974.

Beach for a week's vacation. Before dinner one night in Florida, we watched President Nixon leave the White House, for good. President Ford was sworn in. "That takes care of Watergate," I announced.

But the September smiles hid some bitterness that existed within our party. Some of it was the result of unrealistic hopes for the first Republican state administration in fifty years. A lot was the result of a divisive primary that I was not expected to win. And Republicans had become complacent and forgotten there are more Democrats than Republicans in Tennessee.

One Sunday morning in September Howard Baker called. "What do you think about what Ford has done?"

"What has he done?" I asked.

"Pardoned Nixon," said Baker.

"What will that do?" I asked.

"I'm afraid he's bought the whole problem for all of us," said Howard. Since Howard wasn't running that year, "us" meant me. Voters were disgusted. The Watergate backlash smashed Republicans everywhere. We lost county judges and tax assessors and dropped from having control of the state House of Representatives in 1968 to having only one-third of the members in 1974. And I had the worst vote total of any Republican candidate since our new two-party competition had started. "People we have never seen before are coming out of the mountains to vote against the Republicans," was what I heard from election officials all over the state on election day. I would have to wait awhile to be governor.

"Well, Where's Floyd?" That was the first thing the White County mechanic said when he rolled out from under his car and looked up into my face. It was May 9, 1978. I had walked down from the Cumberland Plateau into the viewing area for Nashville's Channel 4, where I had appeared between 1975 and 1977 twice a week with Floyd Kephart on the six o'clock news. Each debate had been only two minutes long, but three hundred thousand people saw each one.

Those debates had as much to do with my being elected governor in 1978 as Ray Blanton's pardons, Jake Butcher's financial wheeling and dealing, and my walk across the state. For example, I received nearly 60 percent of the vote in Nashville where only 10 percent of the people admit to being Republicans.

Being seen on television gives a candidate, or anyone else, a certain star quality that can help in a campaign. Garrison Keillor of the radio show "A Prairie Home Companion" describes it this way: "If people hear you on the radio, they want to come up and say hello to you. If people see you on television, they want to come up and stare at you."

The way I remind myself that being on television doesn't make me important is to think about the biggest crowd we ever had in Maryville at the Hillbilly Homecoming. It was when Francis the Talking Mule walked in our parade. We had mules all over Blount County, but everyone still wanted to see Francis because *that mule had been on television.*

When You See a Turtle on Top of a Fencepost, You Know He Had Some Help Getting There. Jake Butcher was the fast rabbit in the 1978 campaign; I was the turtle; and campaign manager Tom Ingram and consultant Doug Bailey (along with a host of others) were the ones who helped me get there. One reason Tom and Doug liked my walk across the state was that it put me out on the road for six months, and I was usually having too much fun, or too tired, or too far from a phone booth to call and give much advice about how to run the campaign.

Winning an Election Is a Lot Like Turning Thirteen. When Leslee turned thirteen it was a non-event at our house. She had been looking forward to being thirteen for so long—and we had already suffered and enjoyed the thought of that moment so much—we were ready for something else.

That was the way election night was for me on November 7, 1978. After so many years of pushing and shoving and imposing—and especially after losing in 1974—I was surprised that election night, for me, was so flat. Now I realize that most of the joy of the moment had been used up in anticipation of the event.

But, for thousands of other people, that night was a Big Event. The election night party was so crowded that the security became concerned by the crush at the Opryland Hotel. When I decided to walk out through the crowd, I was nearly knocked down and literally had to push friends out of the way to get to the door.

This was in contrast to four years earlier when I had learned about my defeat from the car radio while driving to our "victory party." Most of our supporters who heard the news then went home. Being a losing candidate at your own victory party on election night must be the closest thing in life to experiencing your own funeral.

When It Came My Time to Say George Bush's Name I Flubbed It. I have been to four Republican National Conventions, twice as chairman of the Tennessee delegation, and the only time I had anything important to do was as a stringer for Nashville's Channel 4 in 1976. I've learned that the major pastime at national political conventions is one reporter interviewing another.

The one great moment for a delegation chairman is the roll call of the states. I can remember lying on the floor at home listening to the Zenith radio in 1948, 1952, and 1956 as delegation after delegation chairman shouted into the microphone some glorious compliment for his state and announced the delegation's vote.

"Mr. Chairman," I began, at the 1980 convention, "the state of Tennessee, home of the nation's proudest volunteers, proudly and unanimously casts its thirty-two votes for *Robert* Bush for vice president of the United States."

You Are Not Likely to See a Picture of Ronald Reagan Campaigning Like This Again. In September 1980, just six and a half weeks before he defeated Jimmy Carter, I drove with Ronald Reagan past several National Guard units on our way to a rally in Knoxville.

"What's the strength of your Guard?" Reagan asked. "How's their morale? We must find a way to improve their prestige in the eyes of all Americans. Years ago, we used to do that with movies. That's hard to do today but the president could help."

He was talking so vigorously that he did not see a group of children who were waving and holding a "Welcome President Reagan" sign. I interrupted him.

"When President Carter was here earlier this year, I talked to a number of children who were disappointed when his motorcade sped past and he didn't wave," I said.

Four years later in Nashville, the president was speeding in his motorcade from the airport to the Opryland Hotel. Several times he asked the driver to slow down so that he could wave at children along the way. "I've never failed to do that since you told me about Jimmy Carter in 1980," he told me. He had remembered our conversation, one I had completely forgotten.

41

I Was Proud to Be Nominated by the Republicans, but I Have Served by the Grace of the Democrats. By the grace of which of these Democrats I can't be sure, but at least we all seem to be singing the same tune here. Choir members included Buddy Killen, Nashville Police Chief Joe Casey, Sheriff Fate Thomas, Senator Jim Sasser, composer Felice Bryant, and Nashville Mayor Richard Fulton. The excuse for the party was the naming of Bryant's song, "Rocky Top," as Tennessee's fifth state song in 1982.

We Raised $1.2 Million in Forty-five Community Days and Left Every Penny of It in the Community Where We Found It.
Before running for a second term in 1982 I asked myself if there was some way not to waste so much money in a reelection campaign and to use the prestige of the governor's office to do some good.

Doug Bailey came up with a super campaign idea—Community Days. Honey and I went where we were invited. We helped turn a superintendent's house at the fish hatchery in Erwin into a local museum, built a senior citizens' center in Loudon, worked all day with five hundred volunteers to clean up a filthy, abandoned school in Memphis so children would have a place to play, and helped Red Bank and Selmer each raise more than one hundred thousand dollars for a football stadium and a library respectively. The impulse for this idea was my growing understanding that most good things happen community by community, not in some

great state plan. Communities—not governors—fix schools. Towns that don't prepare themselves for new industries usually don't get them. Already, the germ of Tennessee Homecoming '86, our community-by-community celebration for the second term, was in our minds.

"There Is One Million Dollars of Butcher Money in Randy Tyree's Campaign." My statement at the Alcoa Kiwanis Club meeting, twelve days before the 1982 election, enraged Sonya Butcher, Jake's wife. She traveled the state, calling me a liar at press conferences. I was tempted to reply to Sonya that Jake simply wasn't telling her everything he was doing, but I was afraid people would think that was a case of a mean governor picking on a defenseless lady. I kept quiet. Jake jumped in anyway to support his wife, and he and Randy kept the "Butcher money" issue alive for the rest of the campaign.

I had guessed about the amount, but my hunch was right according to court records that later showed up. I had learned how to smell Butcher political money in the 1978 campaign. As I walked across the state, I had seen the Butcher campaign buy up whole storefronts and pour thousands of dollars into Memphis black precincts in order to beat Bob Clement in the primary. So in October 1982, when Randy Tyree showed up with a five-hundred-thousand-dollar telephone bank and a solid television buy for the last month, I knew the money had to be Butcher contributions or loans.

I made the charge deliberately, because 1982 was becoming the second worst year for a Republican to run for governor since 1966. (I remembered well the worst year—1974.) The bad economy threatened to sweep thousands of uncommitted and unhappy voters into the Democratic column during the last few days of the campaign. Nationwide, three out of four Republican candidates for governor lost in 1982, and some big-state incumbent Republicans barely squeaked through. In Tennessee the focus on the "Butcher money" stole center stage from the bad economic news and helped me win with about 60 percent of the vote.

A World's Fair Conversation with Jake Butcher in September 1982, About a Month before the Butcher Money Controversy Began. The fair was in many respects successful, and Jake and his business enterprises deserve a great deal of credit. But on Valentine's Day 1983, after a series of all-night telephone calls to Paul Volcker and Federal Reserve and state banking officials, the State Banking Commissioner closed Jake's flagship bank, the United American Bank in Knoxville, the first of twelve Butcher banks to fail.

That evening at the Residence a trooper came to me just before dinner and said, "Jake Butcher's on the phone, Governor, and wants to speak to you."

"I'll bet you're too chicken to take it," Drew said. I answered the phone.

"Lamar, why did you let them do that? Why didn't you give us more time? I thought we could work things out. If Randy had been elected, this never would have happened." Jake and I talked, reasonably and pleasantly, for a few minutes. I haven't spoken to him since.

Jake and Sonya have four fine children who are just a little older than ours. I've thought a lot about the Butchers and gain no joy from their family tragedies.

Don Sundquist

Cissy Baker

Tom Beasley

The Year My Political Advice Was One Hundred Percent Wrong. By 1982 the Democrats in the legislature had mastered computer technology and had created nine weird looking congressional districts designed to elect a maximum number of Democratic congressmen. One of those districts, which resembled a salamander, stretched all the way from Lawrenceburg in Middle Tennessee to Morristown in East Tennessee. I called Cissy Baker, then twenty-five, and said, "This district's made for you. You can win it." During her father's 1966 campaign I had been one of Cissy's babysitters. She took my advice, jumped in the race, and lost two to one.

Meanwhile, I had asked to see Don Sundquist of Memphis, who was considering running for the Republican nomination to succeed Robin Beard in another stretched out district between Nashville and Memphis. "Don, I hate to tell you this," I said, "but you'll never be able to win." Don ran a textbook campaign, defeating Bob Clement in the last ten days, and is now one of the fastest-rising new congressmen in Washington.

The story is not over. My favorite candidate for Don's seat was Tom Beasley, the former Republican state chairman. "This congressional race is your opportunity of a lifetime," I assured Tom. He thought differently and pursued a new idea for private management of prisons. Today he is chairman of Corrections Corporation of America and appears to have made lots of money.

So much for my advice.

Where the Political Action Will Be in the 1990s

In the summer of 1963, between semesters at New York University Law School, I was a law clerk for Bobby Kennedy, the attorney general of the United States. Washington, D.C., was a boiling pot of political action mostly because of the Kennedys. The attorney general drove alone down Constitution Avenue in a blue convertible with the top down, his shock of hair blowing. His shaggy dog, Brumus, wandered with him through the halls of the Department of Justice. Everyone played touch football. This was the age of the young, government-can-do-something, coat-thrown-over-the-shoulder crowd.

When I followed Howard Baker to Washington in 1967, the action still was there. President Lyndon Johnson was using the national government to fight Vietcong and poverty, Lady Bird was using it to plant flowers and ban billboards, and Washington bureaucrats were meddling in the most local of all institutions, the schools. Mayors flew to Washington to discuss things like sewer grants. Washington budget decisions made every city hall tremble. Among Senator Baker's first visitors was a delegation from Maryville, my hometown, wanting federal aid. Well, they didn't really *want* federal aid. They were, in fact, embarrassed to ask for it, as if it were welfare and they were beggars. But they had heard about the Model City money and felt obligated to apply.

The most celebrated politicians of the age were the new young activist senators: Brooke and Percy and Hatfield and Baker and Tower and Mondale and the Kennedy brothers. Governors? Governors were keepers of the provinces, lucky to have their phone calls to Washington answered, unless the name was Reagan or Rockefeller. They were from the two big states, and *they* might run for president one day. People who really counted paid little attention to what went on most other places, in the provinces between New York and California. That was "fly over" country—good only for flying over as one traveled from New York to California. Governors, therefore, rarely were seen on the network evening news, which defined for most people who or what was important in their lives.

Embarrassed by their irrelevance, the governors created a stronger Washington office so they could speak to the real issues, the *Washington* issues. And when the governors met in Washington it was clear many of them had been practicing how to speak on Washington issues in fifteen second sound bites in the hope they might be confused with senators and be shown on the evening news. The governors began to look like one more big public interest lobbying group, which made many governors feel very uncomfortable.

Today, twenty years after my first taste of Washington's glamour I can see the political action shifting to the states. Now governors don't care so much about appearing vivid in Washington terms.

When we met in Washington in February 1986, we spent little time talking like senators. Our most crowded meeting was about local schools. Governors sense the political excitement in *state* capitols. We see the old coalitions breaking down, the ones that unnaturally forced so much attention and money into one central place—instead of just three television networks, there is cable TV; and even the press that prints extra money when Washington needs it has slowed down.

The government-can-do-something, coat-thrown-over-the-shoulder people today are planning assaults to capture the governors' chairs, legislative seats and community offices. That is where the action should be and will be in the 1990s in America.

"Which One Is Governor Lamar?" "And what state is he from?" Those were the two questions Washington television reporters most frequently asked my press secretary John Parish at this press conference on the White House lawn. I was chairman of the National Governors' Association and had just finished meeting with President Reagan. A governor in his own state outranks everyone except the president of the United States. Outside his own state, almost everyone outranks him, which is one reason most governors stay close to home.

EIGHT STORIES

The Day Six Governors Came to Grinder's Switch

Minnie Pearl, our Homecoming Co-chairman, was the cause of it.

There hadn't been, so they said in Centerville, any governor in Grinder's Switch since the fifties when Frank Clement came campaigning, and now, thirty years later, here came six. Not only the governor of Tennessee but Governor Bob Orr of Indiana, Governor Kit Bond of Missouri, Governor Dick Thornburgh of Pennsylvania, Governor Dick Riley of South Carolina, and Governor Scott Matheson of Utah. They were in Nashville for the National Governors Association meeting, and Minnie had brought them all down to show off Homecoming.

As you might expect they traveled like governors—in a bus with patrol cars and helicopters hovering everywhere. (Some people thought there had been a prison break at Turney Center.) The governors wanted their picture taken with Minnie at the Grinder's Switch Depot, the depot being about all there is of the whole place.

Minnie then took them on to the county seat, Centerville, to show why places like Grinder's Switch are important. There are sixty-three communities more or less the size of Grinder's Switch in Hickman County, places like Bon Aqua, Aetna, Lyles, and Only. Every one is important, but a lot of people have forgotten why.

Polly Horner showed us their Heritage quilt. Each patch represents one of those sixty-three communities. The older folks showed the younger folks how to quilt and told them something about each of those communities during the months they worked on it.

The town square in Centerville was full, maybe 2800 people, about everybody who lived there. Every face was smiling and happy, and the sun was shining bright. The speeches were short and Minnie was Minnie and everybody loved it. Governor Orr of Indiana went right home and started Hoosier '88. At last count Indiana had 200 communities signed up because every one of those communities is special, too, just like Grinder's Switch.

My First Inauguration

The metronomic cadence of my new friends marching by was a surprise. After all, these 450 high school juniors had been strangers only six days earlier when they had come to Castle Heights Military Academy in Lebanon from every corner of Tennessee. Their parade lines seemed even more exact because every boy wore blue jeans and a white Boys State T-shirt. A week of mock elections, debates, and athletic contests had pointed to this Saturday ceremony, the inauguration of *our* governor.

At noon the parade music stopped, and the boys collapsed onto rows of folding chairs in front of the high concrete steps beside the drill field. Parents disappeared beneath big white oaks behind the chairs, reluctant to interfere with their suddenly well-disciplined sons.

It was a bright June morning in 1957. Seated on the reviewing platform at the top of the steps, I squinted. Under the oaks I saw my dad's proud smile, as if he had expected this all along. Mother was trying hard not to say too much.

Looking at the rows of blue jeans and white shirts on brown chairs, my eyes caught the eyes of the Chattanooga football player who had come within four votes of winning the right to sit where I sat. A few rows away was the Nashville debater who had fallen seven votes short. In campaign speeches he had perfectly imitated the oratory of Tennessee's real governor, Frank Clement.

When I had boarded the school bus a week ago in Maryville, my bag had been half stuffed with campaign posters announcing my candidacy for governor of Boys State. "Let's Go Far With Lamar," the posters read. I had run them off for eight dollars at Byron's Print Shop. In Alcoa my campaign manager boarded the bus. At the stops in Knoxville and Oak Ridge I gathered more support from the boys who had not heard before that only four Boys State governors ever had been elected from East Tennessee.

My mythical city and party had nominated me. There were campaign visits, campaign debates, and campaign tricks. "The Singing Waiters," two Knoxville delegates with ukulele and banjo, helped draw crowds so I could speak, and they even invented a campaign jingle to the tune of a Brock's candy commercial. I had won the election—barely.

The American Legion had arranged for all of the trimmings that go with an inauguration. There had been an inaugural ball the night before—complete with girls, including the governor of Girls State, a brunette from Springfield. And the real governor of Tennessee was coming to give a speech.

He arrived just as the inaugural parade ended. Sirens squealed in the distance. The Lebanon police chief's car came first, red lights flashing, moving faster than necessary. Then, a limousine swerved through the academy's iron gates, sped up the long driveway, and jerked to a stop in front of the steps where we sat. A highway patrolman opened the right rear door of the limousine, and Governor Clement emerged.

The governor wore a big smile and a big western hat. (Tennesseans in my experience did not wear big western hats. But, then, I'd never before seen a Tennessee governor. *Maybe western hats*, I thought, *like limousines, go with governors*.)

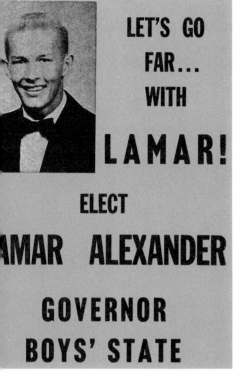

LET'S GO FAR... WITH **LAMAR!** ELECT LAMAR ALEXANDER GOVERNOR BOYS' STATE

The American Legionnaires rushed to the governor, competing to laugh the loudest at his jokes. He walked quickly up the concrete steps to the reviewing stand. His hands shook when he lit a cigarette. He was handsome, but his head seemed too large. The band began the "Star Spangled Banner," and when he took off his western hat, there was a balding spot carefully hidden toward the back of his black hair. Compared to the thinness of seventeen-year-old boys in T-shirts and jeans, he seemed heavy for a young governor. His slick gray suit accentuated his heaviness and his swarthiness. The suit, someone whispered, was shark skin.

We were ready for a real speech. Governor Clement was one of America's great political orators. A year earlier, at the Democratic National Convention, he had delivered his famous line: "How long, oh, how long...?" Someone had told us the governor prepared for a speech by listening on his car radio to an hour of loud gospel music. Then, arriving at the last moment, he would transfer the throbbing beat of the music to the rhythms of his speech. Governor Clement spoke brilliantly and sat down.

Suddenly, the Nashville basketball player who was chief justice asked, "Are you ready to take the oath of office?"

I placed my left hand on the Bible, raised my right hand, and repeated the oath.

Our Boys State counselors had told us all week that the inauguration, more than any other American institution, symbolized the importance of free elections in a democracy. This was a little much for us. At age seventeen we were more interested in Elvis, how our muscles looked when we wore T-shirts, the fidelity of our girlfriends, and the length of our vacations.

It was my turn to speak. The Boys State handbook had said that the inaugural address is "the one speech that will most likely identify you in the minds of the people of your state long after your term has expired." I tried hard to make my remarks memorable. Reading them today, they sound stuffy instead.

The ceremony ended. I quickly said my thanks and good-bys and plunged into the back seat of my parents' Ford, anxious to sleep during the three-hour ride home. Half-awake, half-dreaming I wondered how many of the other boys—riding toward home and remembering the remarkable week of learning about democracy— were thinking about the only sentence of Governor Clement's speech that really had stuck in my mind: "Someday one of you boys is going to grow up to be the real governor of Tennessee."

The Sniper

"We think we've found a sniper in the Hermitage Hotel," Tom Ingram said. "He's in custody, but he may have friends. You'll have to decide whether to go ahead with the inauguration. We think you should, but you need to wear a bulletproof vest."

Until Tom, the chief of staff, told me that, January 14, 1983, had been a great day. Visitors were already arriving for the next day's noon inauguration. In November I had won a big re-election when most Republican candidates for governor had lost. There were no campaign debts. I was proud of the reorganized cabinet. Most important, I would be the first Tennessee governor to serve eight consecutive years, and I had been planning for months to take advantage of it. And this was supposed to be the *happy* inauguration, different from the one four years ago which was marred by the early swearing in.

"What do you mean—a sniper?" I snapped. I was almost ready to blame Ingram for inventing the bad news.

A police sharpshooter perched on top of the Capitol (upper left) at the second inauguration.

"Last night Metro police picked up a man for using stolen credit cards," Tom said. "He had a rifle and a tool box in his room at the Hermitage Hotel. We investigated because the man had written you a threatening letter, and because of comments he had made about you in a book he was writing. The Secret Service was already involved because of earlier letters he wrote to Rosalyn Carter."

I sank in my chair. For four years I had chafed under, and mostly ignored, security restrictions. They had started on election night with Opryland security guards pushing aside my overeager supporters, Williamson County deputies sleeping in the den, and highway patrolmen driving the family everywhere we went. I even caught myself taking my frustration out on the tolerant troopers who did their best to stay out of the way in a job that paid them to be in the way. I had been elected after walking across the state; I did not like hiding from the people.

"Here is what else we found," Tom continued.

"In addition to the rifle and tool box, we found a snub-nosed .38

Smith and Wesson pistol with hollow point bullets in his room; the room did not face the Legislative Plaza where the inaugural will be, but with the tools he could easily have broken into other rooms or gained access to the hotel roof; he had a passport application and an account book showing recent deposits of several thousand dollars; he had an airline ticket from Nashville to Washington for a time just after you are supposed to attend an event at the Hyatt today; we also found an address book with a number of unusual entries like the French Embassy, the Soviet Embassy, WNGE-TV, airlines, credit card offices, the names of various public officials, both here and abroad."

I knew that governors received threats. I had heard Governor Ellington tell governor-elect Dunn in 1970 that he was going to build an iron fence around the Governor's Residence because a man had wandered in the front door one day with a loaded pistol. Threatening letters came to me too, but I never read them. The only time I had become concerned was when a woman, who had threatened our children, appeared one Sunday sitting in the pew directly behind us at church. My plans for the Saturday inauguration had been to put on my red and black shirt and kick off "Tennessee Homecoming '86" with the inaugural parade, not to shrink within a bulletproof vest and avoid the people I was elected to serve.

Saturday morning was clear and cold. I looked from the front row of the inaugural platform across the brightly colored hats of several hundred tightly bundled onlookers, across the Legislative Plaza to the Hermitage Hotel. Today it seemed taller than usual. As the ceremony proceeded it sometimes seemed like the only building on the square. The bulletproof vest filled my black raincoat like shoulder pads under a football uniform, but no one seemed to notice. I saw every trooper and special agent I knew dressed in plain clothes and spaced among the dignitaries, on the platform, in the crowd, wherever we walked. In the shadows around the top of the Capitol behind me I saw police sharpshooters. *What if someone does fire a rifle and misses me, hitting our children, hitting anyone? Should I stop the ceremony just to be safe*, I wondered.

I hurried through my address. The twenty-one consecutive cannon shots ending the ceremony seemed like a one-hundred-twenty-one-gun salute. I left the stage quickly and changed clothes, draping a loose red and black jacket over my newly broadened shoulders, and walked to the head of the inaugural parade. Away from the Plaza I felt more relaxed, but I was glad when the day ended.

I have put the sniper suspect—who is still in jail on other charges—and most other security considerations out of my mind. My official schedule during the second term has been like the first: open meetings, public events, walking in lots of parades. I finally agreed to having a highway patrol car follow mine, to putting bulletproof glass in the window just behind my desk at the Capitol, and installing electronic eyes at the Residence.

I have taken the oath of office as governor three times, and the first time and the last time were two of the hardest days of my life.

Washboard Playing On Bourbon Street

I was the trombone player at Your Father's Moustache in New Orleans when I was law clerk to John Minor Wisdom. The truth is, I was the *substitute* trombone player when I was Judge Wisdom's *messenger*. In 1965 U.S. Court of Appeals judges only had one law clerk, and I had grabbed the Fifth Circuit Court's messenger job, even at three hundred dollars per month, because Judge Wisdom had promised to treat me like a real law clerk and my New York University law professors had assured me that Judge Wisdom was one of the best federal judges in America.

The judge was true to his word. From the day I moved into an upstairs apartment on Felicity Street—not far from the Wisdom mansion in the Garden District—I was one of the family. He offered advice about my date for Mardi Gras. The judge's wife, Bonnie, made sure I learned how to confront an artichoke and instructed me that dinner was *always* promptly at 6:00 and that *mous*tache was pronounced mous*tache*.

Your Father's Moustache, whatever its pronunciation, was a Bourbon Street bar. It featured a banjo band of young men wearing red-gartered shirts and straw hats and an atmosphere heavily influenced by beer, peanuts, and rowdy singing. It was not a dangerous place—except occasionally, such as when teams of women bowlers convened in New Orleans and, after a few beers, rushed the band members, somewhat akin to what was going on across the street at the corner night club where Linda Some-body was fending off the male customers during *her* performance. I was the front line of defense against the charging women bowlers, thrusting my trombone slide as a bayonet, in between choruses of "Mississippi Mud" and "It's a Grand Old Flag," urging them back toward the tables. On Tuesdays through Saturdays I played for whoever was off: one night it was for the trombone player, one for the tuba, one for the piano, and two for the washboard.

I preferred the trombone, because it drowned out everything

else, but it was the washboard—played with an old spoon—that Judge Wisdom liked best. And it was the washboard that I was strumming the night he cajoled and pushed the entire U.S. Fifth Circuit Court of Appeals to sit in the very front row, between the singing college students and the blaring band, perfectly positioned *en banc* in the midst of roaring crosscurrents of noise. Whether the other judges had fun, I have no idea, but I could tell Judge Wisdom did.

Judge Wisdom, in fact, had lots of fun. His afternoon absences from his chambers in the Wildlife and Fisheries Building on Royal Street—just a block or two from Your Father's Moustache—were, I discovered after a few months, to visit his club to play bridge. He had been an enthusiastic Mardi Gras participant, but he gave up riding carnival floats after becoming a judge. He said it was not because of what people might suspect about his condition should he fall off one of the floats, but because they would probably be correct in their suspicions.

He had fun too, with his highly successful law practice, especially with the big cases. And he had great fun being a Republican. He loved recounting how he and fellow Judge John Brown had taken over the Louisiana and Texas delegations and helped to throw the 1952 Republican convention to Ike. He was a big enough Republican that Richard Nixon had visited his home in 1966. The two men disappeared for thirty minutes into the study; none of us knows yet what secrets they swapped, but it must not have been the Supreme Court seat that we clerks thought the judge had earned but never came his way.

My professors were right about John Wisdom's being a great judge; he had fun doing that, too. He loved working with words, trying them one way, then another, laboring endlessly. He enjoyed being the guest of honor at the annual banquet of the *Yale Law Journal*—where I first had heard him speak—and liked playing the role of a southerner with the northern Seal of Approval, even though the same progressive opinions that earned northern approval repelled many of his friends at his club, in his neighborhood, and in his old krewe.

During the last twenty years, since I graduated from the "College of Wisdom," I have worked with all sorts of men and women in high places. Many were so narrow-gauged that they couldn't discern a human frailty or need if it smashed them in the face. Some of my friends in the Nixon White House were like that. On the other hand, the broad-gauged people, the ones who had lived and grown and fought and been defeated in a variety of life's arenas—men like Bryce Harlow, Arthur Burns, Pat Moynihan, and Henry Kissinger—survived very well. Still others with whom I have worked, many of whom were trained at the best schools and who edited the finest law reviews and whose credentials were perfect, could perform mental gymnastics of intimidating olympic quality, but when faced with a decision, couldn't make one worth two cents.

Judge Wisdom fought political wars, rode carnival floats, played at clubs, and found his way deep into the hearts and the lives of his friends. Nearly one hundred of us who were Wisdom law clerks can swear to that. His brilliance, integrity, and precision have been models for us, but so has been his broad-gauged life. To us it makes sense that the judge who knew enough about life to convene the U.S. Court of Appeals *en banc* to hear his favorite washboard player was also the judge who ordered Governor Ross Barnett to admit James Meredith to Ole Miss.

Reprinted by permission of the *Tulane Law Review*

Sliding into First

She slid into first base, but it was her bright red shorts that got my attention. Honey still denies sliding into first base, but she did. And the slide, plus her bright red shorts, sent me reeling. We were playing in a staff softball game in Washington, D.C., during the summer of 1967. I was on Senator Baker's team, and the girl in the red shorts played on the team of Senator John G. Tower of Texas. After seeing Honey for the first time, I began to play softball the way a peacock struts through the farmyard. My first at bat resulted in a line drive over the left fielder's head, and I turned it into a home run. (She must have noticed that.) My second hit was a flat-out home run. (There!) My pitches were mostly good strikes. (I knew Texas girls appreciated great athletes.) Then I hit a triple. Then another home run. Senator Baker's team tromped Senator Tower's team, and we proceeded to the event for which the late afternoon softball game was merely the excuse: the after-game staff party.

For the next eighteen months Honey Buhler and I courted and enjoyed Washington. As senate aides we saw Washington up close, often at its best: Everett Dirksen, the Republican leader, charming visitors in packed Senate galleries with his annual speech urging that the marigold be the national flower; John Tower and Hubert Humphrey, railing at each other about labor legislation and then embracing and walking arm-in-arm off the Senate floor as happy as any two good friends; Mike Mansfield, the Democratic leader, spare and pipe-smoking, answering reporters' questions with a "Yep" and a "Nope" and a "Don't know" and getting away with it.

On January 4, 1969, while I was out of a job but hoping for a Nixon White House appointment, Honey and I were married in Victoria, Texas. Senator Tower was there, still watching out for his softball team.

My Most Embarrassing Moment As Governor

A cold morning rain had made mud out of the pasture Maymee Cantrell used to own, and the dignitaries' car wheels were plowing the mud into furrows. Nissan officials had put up a large tent in the center of the pasture to shelter the groundbreaking ceremony and to ward off the rain and chill. And I had ordered fifty state troopers to be on hand to ward off the trouble. There were enough rumors of trouble that some of the Democratic leaders had stayed in their offices at the Legislative Plaza. It was February 3, 1981.

When I sloshed through the mud into the tent I realized that fifty state troopers were not one too many. I had expected to see rows of proud civic leaders, their faces beaming because of the worldwide attention focused on their hometown. Nissan had selected Smyrna for Japan's largest overseas investment. Instead, the audience was a threatening mob of noisy men, standing, chanting, obviously determined to stop the ceremony. I finally spotted the community leaders standing along the edge of the tent, shivering in raincoats, as if they had been shoved to the side. In the middle of the noisy crowd a dozen television cameras were mounted like a row of machine guns aimed at the platform where I was to sit with Nissan, state, and local officials.

Marvin Runyon, the Nissan president, was determined to go ahead with the ceremony, and I was determined to support him. The union demonstrators were mad because Nissan was using a construction company that hired both union and nonunion workers. Ninety-five percent of all construction work in Middle Tennessee is done by such "merit shop" contractors, and Tennessee has a right-to-work law that permits employees to choose whether to join a union or not. To let rowdies cancel this groundbreaking would be a signal that our laws meant nothing.

Runyon welcomed the crowd. The crowd booed and shouted, "Jap, go home." Mayor Sam Ridley, himself a bomber pilot in World War II, offered a fervent welcome to the Japanese company. The shouts of the crowd grew louder. When Masataka Okuma, the seventy-year-old ranking Nissan official from Tokyo responded, his hands trembled from the cold, but his voice was steady. I wondered what he must be thinking. I wondered how I would have felt in Nagasaki or Hiroshima, the only American in a crowd of belligerent Japanese workers crowding close and chanting, "Yankee, go home."

When my turn came, the demonstrators were in full voice. I could either denounce them or let their obnoxious conduct speak for itself. I knew something they did not: the microphone in front of me fed sound to all twelve television cameras. Their rude shouts could drown my voice in Smyrna, but the world would still hear on the evening news what I had to say. I welcomed Nissan with these words:

> It would be hard to overestimate the importance of this new facility to the state of Tennessee. Nissan is one of the three or four leaders in what is becoming a global industry. Having their United States headquarters here will not only be of tremendous direct value to us but will also be a magnet for other high-technology industries from around the nation and around the world.

> Twenty years ago, Mel Tillis sang a great country song, "Detroit City," about the thousands of southerners who had to leave home to find jobs in the assembly plants and factories in the North. Now, thanks to Nissan, many members of the present generation can stay here and get those high-paying jobs, and some of the ones who had to go away before can come back home. That's not cause for protest. It's cause for celebration.

The demonstrators made so much noise that it was hard to tell when the ceremony ended. Runyon and I, escorted by state troopers, pushed through the mob, past the row of television cameras, to the front of the tent where he was to drive forward a Nissan pickup truck. The demonstrators had deflated and slashed the truck's tires and stuck union bumper stickers on the windows. Runyon drove the truck anyway, amidst a chorus of catcalls from the demonstrators and a few cheers from the now aroused civic leaders.

When Runyon stopped, the demonstrators surrounded the truck and us. The state troopers offered me a clear path out, back through the tent, the way I had entered. But I walked out through the demonstrators. I wanted them to know they could not intimidate me or the state. It was not yet noon, but I smelled whiskey on some of them. I stepped over nails. I saw some knives. I heard ugly comments about the Japanese. Several said, "We're surprised at you, Lamar."

I had never been more disgusted or embarrassed. After all the work by so many people to bring good jobs and good publicity to a state that so badly needed both, a few loudmouths—many from out of state—were messing it up. What would officials in Tokyo think? Had Nissan put its $500 million in the wrong state? And what would other Japanese and American companies think about putting their investment dollars in Tennessee?

The demonstration made news all over the world. Nissan executive Mitsuya Goto appeared on the front page of his hometown Yokohama newspaper, smiling and holding up a sign saying, "Boycott Datsun." The media in both countries had a field day: "Labor demonstration mars largest-ever Japanese plant opening in Tennessee."

59

Tennesseans were outraged. Within one day the legislature unanimously condemned the demonstration as "unrepresentative of Tennesseans," reiterated its bipartisan welcome for Japanese investment, and apologized for what had happened. The legislators' indignation was mild compared to the disgust that dripped from the voices of telephone callers to the local radio talk shows. Tennesseans are proud of their hospitality to strangers. Letters poured into the Nissan offices in Smyrna and Tokyo from embarrassed Tennessee citizens. Newspapers condemned the action. The state AFL-CIO, especially Bruce Thrasher of the United Steelworkers, moved quickly to repair the extensive damage to the union's image, even though the steelworkers had had nothing to do with the demonstration.

When I traveled to Japan later that year, I was relieved to find the Japanese casting a characteristically long view toward the whole situation, correctly understanding it as a one-time episode instigated by a few disappointed unionists. While the experience was painful and rude, Nissan could not have purchased that much good will with all the money in Japan.

II Timothy 2:15

Every time I was sworn in as governor I opened the old Alexander family Bible to II Timothy 2:15. It was my father's favorite Bible verse. He would recite it when we children memorized verses; sometimes he included it in his letters when I was away at school: "Study to show thyself approved unto God. A workman that needeth not to be ashamed, rightly dividing the word of truth."

"Why does that verse mean so much to you?" I asked him more than once. "I've just known it since I was a boy," was all he ever said.

In 1979 the Billy Graham Crusade came to Nashville. I was asked to play the piano for the singing. The crowd of thirty-five thousand warmed up a hot June evening even more when Cliff Barrows, Dr. Graham's song leader, led the singing and I played the nine-foot Steinway on the stage in the center of Vanderbilt stadium.

Playing that night reminded me of my boyhood, when Dad led the singing and I played the piano at revivals. I knew the gospel hymns by heart and liked to jazz them up the way I heard them on early Sunday morning radio shows. I told Dad that if we only had a tent and someone to pass the collection plate we could go on the road.

Dad's love for singing went back to *his* boyhood. His father's farm was next door to the National Campground near Loudon. Since 1873, families had been coming there for week-long meetings to hear strong preaching and to join in good singing. "Let everybody sing like we're getting the clothes off the line in a hard shower," was the way they went at it. On August nights Dad could hear the singing, even when he wasn't at the camp meetings.

"The Alexanders have always had a lot of music in them and

good voices," Dad—who sang tenor—would say. "One of our cousins, Charles M., the sheriff's son from down in Meadow, got to be a famous song leader, known all over the world."

"Are you any relation to Charles M. Alexander?" Cliff Barrows had asked me the night before the Graham crusade. We were at a "get-acquainted session," which I assumed was a polite way of finding out whether I really could play the piano. When I told him that Charles M. Alexander was Dad's older cousin and had grown up on a nearby farm, Barrows' face brightened: "He was the world's greatest song leader at the turn of the century," he said. "He studied under Dwight Moody, traveled with Billy Sunday, and went around the world to England, Australia, and even Japan with R. A. Torrey. He did then what I do today, and no one has inspired me more.

"Those meetings drew crowds of thousands," Barrows continued. "And Charles M. Alexander was the one who brought them to their feet, singing their hearts out."

A month after the Nashville crusade ended Barrows sent me one of his two books about Charles M. Alexander's life. I turned the pages at random, from back to front. There were pictures from 1903 of crowds in Kyoto, in Shanghai, and in Melbourne, stories of singing and soul winning—and of growing up in Blount County and attending Maryville College.

When I found the book's front page, I stared at it. There was his signature, written just like this:

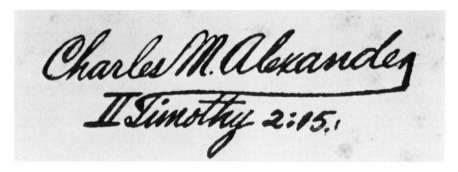

In 1895, II Timothy 2:15 had been his "year-text" and, afterward he had always signed his name that way even though Dad must have never known it.

On the Way to Nashville
On Air Force One

From my notes, September 13, 1984:
- Television crews at Andrews Air Force Base photograph everyone boarding Air Force One. Why? "So they'll have pictures in case the plane crashes," I'm told.
- White House photographs decorate the inside of the plane: the president and the pope, with the pope waving; the president and Michael Jackson, with Michael Jackson waving. Some of the president's staff and I joke about getting off

the plane, waving, with Michael Jackson gloves on only our right hands.

- The president walks from his private compartment in the front to our compartment for a visit. He tells five good stories in a row. Like all good storytellers, he has a good supply, and it makes little difference either to him or to his listeners whether he has told them before.

- The president is wearing jogging pants. When he's flying he takes off his suit so it doesn't get wrinkled. He wears clothes not to cover himself but to look good.
- Just before we land in Nashville, I walk to the back of the plane to use the bathroom. As I return, the door to the plane's middle compartment has been shut. When I open it, the room is full of secret service men with their shirts off, putting on bulletproof vests and looking like deliberate young men going to war.
- The president's black limousine has already been flown ahead to Nashville. The glass in its windows is three inches

thick. Interior lights can be turned on so people can see the president when he waves back to them. Behind the limousine are two follow-up cars with automatic submachine guns mounted to the floor. A surface-to-air missile is also available which could knock down a helicopter if it came too close.

- At Opryland Hotel the president stops at a washroom before lunch with Howard Baker, Jim Baker, and me. He tells this story about his race for governor in California: "A doctor had come up to me after I had shaken 250 hands. The doctor told me, 'Do you realize that is the easiest way to catch the flu or some other sort of disease, hand-to-mouth?' Now I always wash my hands after I shake hands," the president says. He washes his hands. We all wash our hands loyally.

- The president's lunch, like his limousine, has also been flown from Washington. So has the waiter from the White House mess, who serves the president his lunch. The waiter was there when I worked in the White House in 1969.

- The president drops by to see Roy Acuff at Roy's Opryland apartment.

"Did George (Bush) give you that photograph I gave him, the picture of the New York marquee, taken about 1948 when I was on the stage and one of your movies was there at the same time?" Roy asks.

"Wasn't the movie *Tennessee Partners*?" the president asks.

"What I remember," Roy says, "is on that marquee I had top billing—Roy Acuff came first and Ronald Reagan second—probably the last time that ever happened!"

FAMILY IN THE GOLDFISH BOWL

by Honey Alexander

Eight years is a long time, a very long time in the life of a young family. We've moved through the normal passages of life, but in the public eye. Growth and change, change and growth. Those two words sum up the past eight years.

When we moved into the grand Executive Residence, it was spic and span, but a threadbare museum of American antiques. There was no life and little depicting Tennessee. We arrived with three small children, dogs, guinea pigs, bikes, toys, and, most important, hopes to make this a real home. We wanted it to be a fine home, a place in which Tennesseans could take pride, a place open to everyone, not just our political friends, a place full of Tennessee too. So we pulled up the worn carpets and saw the beautiful black and white marble tiles and hardwood floors. Down came the shredded draperies. In came the light.

For eight years, the Residence has been our official home, a comfortable yet elegant home through which thousands of Tennesseans, Japanese, Texans, Englishmen—all kinds and shapes and sizes and ages and nationalities of people have toured, been fed, been entertained, and done business. There's the Greeneville dining room filled with early East Tennessee furniture and Tennessee silver, paintings, and crafts. Bikes are often seen on the front "stoop"; children are often seen in the pool and the sandbox. There is a lived-in quality and appearance. That's as we want and need it.

It is also easy to see change and growth in the grounds of the Executive Residence. On his first visit back early in Lamar's first term, Winfield Dunn asked about his plum tree. It wasn't where he had planted it. Did I know what had happened to it? I couldn't tell him. Little did I know that I too would become attached to the soil and the growing things of this place—to watching and tending the rose garden, to lamenting the storm that took the enormous white

65

oak on the front lawn. Lightning struck, traveling down the trunk. No matter how much we hoped the oak would survive, it was not to be. The day they came to cut it down, I think all of us—gardeners, children, custodians, security officers, Lamar and me—had tears in our eyes.

Growth and change can also be counted in litters of puppies and kittens and guinea pigs. Animals make children (and their parents) happy. Pets give kids love, demand responsibility, and teach lessons about life. Squire and Sandy moved with us to the Residence. Squire was an English setter who loved to run. One day the gate was cracked just enough for him to squeeze through. One of the highway patrolmen assigned to our staff found him dead on Franklin Road. We had a burial service in the pet graveyard that afternoon. Lots of tears, and a lesson about the pain of death. Sandy was half cocker spaniel, half Pekingese. During a big storm Sandy just disappeared. We called and called and called. Searched and searched and searched. Never a sign.

Molly is Kathryn's black cat. We all learned a lot by watching Molly bear and care for three litters of kittens. Corfe, an English cocker spaniel, is *my* dog, my constant shadow. Lamar gave him to me in the fall of 1981, saying he thought I "needed a friend." Because we had visited England the summer before and had loved climbing on the broken walls of Corfe Castle, we named him Corfe. He was such an agreeable, calm, loyal, fun fellow that a couple of years later we searched the country and found a suitable

Tree trimming around here always comes early in order to have the Residence ready for Christmas tours that start after December 1. Every year the children seemed to be less interested in having Christmas during Thanksgiving. Consequently, the "grumps" in us would come out—and one of the biggest areas of controversy was over who got to use the ladder the most.

Photographer Robin Hood encouraged Kathryn and Corinne Barfield, then age five, to put some of the spring flowers at the Residence in their hair. Look at the results.

Since I was nursing him, Will attended the International Year of the Child meeting with me in Washington, D.C., in July 1979. During this conference, my sister's car broke down and had to be left where it was parked . . . at the vice president's house. How embarrassing!

67

Carrying the Olympic torch through the UT-Knoxville campus was a real thrill. May 1984.

Roan Mountain State Park has terrific cross-country skiing. Eddie Williams introduced us to the sport in the middle of a snowstorm in 1983. It was glorious!

Drew, at the first inauguration, 1979.

When Drew gets into a project, he goes the extra mile. As Lamar and I watched him keeping up with election night results, we saw a lot of his Granddad Alexander in him, both being intent and thorough about those facts and figures. November 1982.

Drew is an enthusiastic, and errat-
ic, tennis player. We enjoy playing
together. I think he and his friend
Patrick Keeble beat Governor Nigh
of Oklahoma handily in this 1984
National Governors' Conference
match.

Drew and Lamar have enjoyed fishing in many of the lakes and streams of
Tennessee. They even went to fly fishing school together one summer. In this
photo, Drew has probably enticed his dad into fishing so that Drew can come out
ahead, one more time!

Leslee's a real soft touch on her
dad, as this 1979 photo shows.
Can't you just hear her saying, "I
luv ya, Daddy"?

A conversation one evening:
"Dad, will you carry me to bed?"
"I'm almost asleep, Leslee."
"Pretty soon I'll be too big for you
to carry me."
Lamar did and today she is.

They look alike (Drew and Leslee).

We are alike (Honey and Leslee).

mate. We named her Lady Diana since it was soon after the Royal Wedding. Now Corfe and Lady bring us new lessons in growth and change. The first litter was born "early" according to the vet, but Leslee and I handled the midwifery without a hitch. And weren't we all proud parents of those adorable puppies?!

Drew was "into chickens" one year, but the dogs weren't sure that even this place was big enough for chickens, too. One day in a flurry of feathers and a choir of squawks, the rooster was "done away with." We searched high and low for the remains so we could have a proper burial. Not a sign. But in the late evening I heard a crow! And then he came. Embarrassed about losing so many of his beautiful feathers, he slinked back into the yard in the near dark. If any of his tail had been left, it would have been tucked between his legs for sure!

Family photos reveal the growth and change in the children since Lamar took office. From the ages of four, six, and nine, Kathryn, Leslee, and Drew have attained the ripe old ages of twelve, fourteen, and seventeen. Eight years *is* a very long time in the life of a young family.

Will has spent all of his seven years with the Executive Residence as home. But he's seen a lot of the world, and if he were writing a book, it would be entitled "Will's Book about His Traveling around the United States—and Other Countries." He has been from Maine's rocky shores to the white sand beaches of the Grand Cayman Island to the pyramids of the Yucatan Peninsula. He has explored the Teton Mountains, Yellowstone Park, Dinosaur National Monument, and the Craters of the Moon National Monument. He's grown through these travels and loved them all. He needs to write that book.

While Will's history of travels may not be "normal" for all seven-year-olds, twelve-year-old Kathryn says that her life has been very normal, with some few exceptions. Certainly, the removal of her appendix was anything but normal. But she handled it all in stride except that her "security pillow"—a very worn, torn, almost-empty-of-feathers baby pillow—got lost in the operating room and was not there to comfort her thereafter. Although I tried to find a substitute, nothing would do until a Chinese "Immigrant Doll," dressed in red silk, found a way into her life five years later. Kathryn has changed and grown from a shy four-year-old, whom we called "Honey's appendage" (because she spent so much time on my hip) into a much more self-assured twelve-year-old with a real mind of her own. She loves her theatre class, runs like a flash, and can't decide whether to teach English or become a doctor when she grows up.

As a self-possessed and independent fourteen-year-old, Leslee still has the bubbling and assertive character that was a major part of her personality eight years ago. She's quite at ease whether jumping fences on horseback or piloting a sailboat. Her fondest recollections of life in the public eye are quite simple: moving to the Residence, traveling, and "all the people I have met." "Such as who?" "Well, the people who work here." She's learned a lot

Leslee was no bigger than the saddle the first time we saw her ride in a show. Her horse slipped, dumping her in the mud. Now she's a good rider, wins lots of ribbons, and spends hours tending Spring, the Texas pony my father gave her.

Leslee, in a pioneer woman's hat, with our English cocker spaniel, Corfe, waited for us on the rainy Sunday morning in Cades Cove when we completed a three-day pilgrimage along the settlers' trail.

All of the children share Lamar's love for music, although their tastes are running to rock right now. Here Cyndy B. Waters has caught Kathryn at the keyboard during a quieter time.

Kathryn, off on her own at Hilton Head Island, 1986.

When we received the invitation for Will to be one of Santa's elves in Nashville's Christmas Parade in December 1985, I almost didn't ask him if he wanted to do it since he has disliked being in crowds and in the public eye. But he was thrilled—and went through the entire day like a political pro!

We have always had lots of animals. Sandy was a favorite of Kathryn's and came with us to live at the Residence as a little puppy. She disappeared during a violent thunderstorm which tore up huge hemlocks by their roots.

hryn said her stomach hurt. ar thought it was all the icy ks and popcorn she ate at the nds game. Fortunately, I took to Vanderbilt Children's Hos- l where doctors removed her endix two hours later.

"Whadya mean a fast ball? I only throw spitballs with my left hand." Will, age eighteen months.

Will has contributed muscle power and thought to our vegetable gardens over the years. Here he and Justin Minor are planting Will's garden of yard-long beans, Indian corn, carrots, sunflowers, pumpkins, and watermelons. Another thing Will has liked about the garden is the okra, which he and Lamar pick, cut, dip in milk and cornmeal, and fry. It's delicious!

from *everyone* but finds simple things please her most: animals (she still has a guinea pig in her room), a beautiful day, pretty things. A real young lady!

From just over four feet four inches in 1978 to almost six feet today, Drew at seventeen has turned into a young man. He still looks back fondly on the times he walked with his father during the 1978 campaign. I remember his reaction to visiting Wilder Youth Center. "It's nice there, Mom. Probably nicer than what any of those boys have at home. A good gym, a room all their own." And he has been quite an entrepreneur too, from selling eggs and Xeroxed copies of his father's signature to legislators (I don't think he made a penny!), to collecting rocks and coins and swapping Grateful Dead tapes. He always enters a new endeavor 150 percent. His longest commitment, though, has been to the guitar: four years of rock blasting from amplified speakers. He's pretty good too!

Before Lamar was elected, I asked him many times, "Why do you want to be governor?" I knew he had the ability and ambition to be a good governor, a great governor, but what was it that he wanted to accomplish?

Now, after eight years of on-the-job training, he can explain that clearly: better schools, healthy children, clean and safe communities, proud Tennesseans. He is enthusiastic and optimistic and better able than ever before to lead people into his vision of this great state, its people, its land, its heritage, and its future.

Being a good governor *is* important to him. He has enjoyed and learned from it. But also important are making sure that his children know he loves them, that we find time to spend together

Will was entranced by the Christmas music during our holiday tours. The house and the crowds got to be too much for him though. Shortly after this photo was taken, he asked if he could come to the party. I told him yes, but he would have to be polite and talk to people when they talked to him. His response was, "I no need go." And he hasn't made many appearances since then.

as a family, that he doesn't let the busyness of life take away opportunities for reflection and observation, that life's simple pleasures don't pass him by. He's good at taking breaks: a pet store visit with Will, a Girl Scout campout with Kathryn, watching Leslee show her horse, fishing with Drew, or listening to "A Prairie Home Companion" on Saturday evenings. He has a good balance to his life.

And me? Lamar and this position of First Lady have stretched my expectations for myself. Now I'm making more speeches, running more meetings, traveling farther. I even completed an Outward Bound course. My experiences have been broadening. My horizons are less limited. But I'm not trying to be Superwoman.

Do we look like Tennessee tourists arriving at Selfridge's Hotel in London before setting out for the Peterborough Country Music Festival?

There are lots of days when the children's rooms don't look perfect and neither do I. I feel much less compelled to weed the gardens or clean the garage myself—I'd really rather be jogging! And the most important facets of my life remain the same: supporting Lamar, mothering the children, helping others, nurturing good physical, spiritual, emotional, and intellectual health in me and in those closest to me.

Growth and change, change and growth. We have all enjoyed and learned from these eight years. We are grateful for the challenges and the opportunities and especially for the support of family and friends. They have made life in the goldfish bowl not only possible and bearable but sometimes wonderful as well.

ODDS 'N' ENDS

Most scrapbooks I've seen usually have a bulge where photographs, newspaper clippings, and assorted memorabilia of every type are being held until the "proper place" for each item can be found. Why should a governor's scrapbook be any different? I have some odds 'n' ends that haven't fit anywhere else in this book, but I think they are worth remembering.

Take this photograph of Honey with President Reagan. It was taken at a dinner when the Reagans were overnight guests at Howard and Joy Baker's home in Huntsville. Are they discussing international terrorism, the national debt, or Nicaragua? No telling. At one White House dinner he explained to her what it was like to kiss an actress while making a movie.

Here are some other "extras" I don't want to forget.

My Favorite Quotes

"I wouldn't like to be governor. I don't like to sign drivers' licenses." KATHRYN ALEXANDER, nine.

"Children and their grandparents get along so well because they have a common enemy." ALEX HALEY.

"Aim for the top. It's less crowded there." R. R. RANKIN, my grandfather.

"In this life you have to be mighty careful where you aim, because you're likely to get there." CHET ATKINS's best advice.

"I've gotten to the point in life where I've decided that if people aren't nice, they're not so hot in my book, no matter how big they are." MINNIE PEARL's best advice.

"I know how hard it is to clap with your fingers crossed." RONALD REAGAN to the Washington press club.

"I want to go home. I've been on a trip here for about a month. I'm sick of Maine. Maine's boring." DREW ALEXANDER, thirteen, to the Portland, Maine, reporter who asked how he liked the Governors' Conference in Portland.

"You didn't!" DREW ALEXANDER'S MOTHER, upon reading the Portland newspaper.

"The wives of politicians deserve a trust fund for their part in campaigning, not to mention those five minute speeches they are called upon to give when they represent their husbands. Plus a bonus for every speech they've heard eighty-five times and remained awake." ERMA BOMBECK.

"Governor Blanton had his one day and I have 364. I'll still be writing when Blanton is in jail." JOHN PARISH, writing in his *Jackson Sun* daily column in May 1977, the day after Ray Blanton said at the Humboldt Strawberry Festival that the Parish column should be used for bird cages.

"I was wrong." JOHN PARISH, in 1985 when he was not writing his column and Blanton was in jail.

"Getting elected is 90 percent brains and 50 percent dumb luck." JACK KEMP.

"There are no issues. My opponent has a job, and I want it. That's what this election is all about." WILLIAM J. BULAR, running for governor of South Dakota in 1926.

When we saw the "Hee Haw" girls, Leslee, ten, and Kathryn, eight, stared speechless. Their wide eyes seemed to ask . . . "Will we look like that when we grow up? And if we do, what will we do?"

Superlatives

For practicing what he teaches: To Professor W. Harry Feinstone at Memphis State University who gave $625,000 of his own money to match $625,000 tax dollars to create the state's first "Chair of Excellence," in molecular biology, at Memphis State.

For coming from nowhere to first place in the shortest period of time: Whitewater rafting on the Ocoee River outside Chattanooga, the most popular river rafting trip in America with nearly one hundred thousand visitors a year. In 1976 there were no trips, and there was even no whitewater until TVA closed an old flume line for repairs and the extra water in the river produced the rapids.

For getting the most out of a name change: To Memphis for dumping its city slogan "Uniport"—which conjures up images of a flying bicycle—in favor of "America's Distribution Center."

The best little project I wish I had thought of in time to get done: Build one thousand miles of bicycle trails across Tennessee.

The best little project I did think of in time to help get done: Restoring the bluebird population to Tennessee by creating a trail of bluebird houses across the state, sort of a homecoming for birds whose homes disappear as fields turn into subdivisions and farms turn into highways.

The most-frequent-visitor-at-the-governor's-residence award goes to...John Austin Echols! John Austin has visited us more than any Japanese businessman, Republican county chairman, or cabinet member. He is part of the family. John and Will race big wheels downstairs on the black and white marble floors, build block railroads that run the length of the upstairs hall, and play "hide and seek" in the State Dining Room. They give the "Children Playing" sign at the driveway some real meaning.

At our cabin in Miller's Cove they ride the big swing on the white oak, slide on smooth rocks in Hesse Creek, and play games on the porches, even in the rain. It makes us happy just to see them so happy.

A typical press conference in the governor's office with a member of the Capitol Hill press corps in the foreground.

The most amazing political spectacle: John Jay Hooker, Jr., and Winfield Dunn crisscrossing the state together five weeks before the election in 1978 in order to gain one million signatures to stop then Governor Blanton from pardoning Roger Humphreys.

More amazing: Blanton did it anyway, after the election.

The best question by a politician visiting the Governor's Residence: "Is the front of the Governor's Mansion in the front, or is the back the front?" by John Jay Hooker, Jr. He's right. It's hard to tell.

One important mistake I made: Promising during the 1978 campaign to open cabinet meetings to the press. Open cabinet meetings proved to be so useless that we quit having them. Instead we worked in private in cabinet councils on jobs, social services, and safe growth. Senior government executives need times to think out loud without being embarrassed. Usually when you think out loud, you later want to take back 80 percent of what you said. But if you *don't* think out loud, you rarely create the good ideas that come from the 20 percent of your out loud thinking that makes sense.

Another mistake: Thinking that cabinet members needed to be specialists in their areas. It is more important that they be leaders and listeners.

My greatest disappointment as governor: When the Master Teacher Program was (temporarily) defeated by one vote in March 1983. I felt then, as I do today, that its success is the key to Tennessee's opportunity to become the kind of state most Tennesseans want.

My greatest failure: Not finding a way to work better with the Tennessee Education Association.

Courtesy of *The Knoxville Journal*

Never Seen before in the Same Campaign and Never to Be Seen Again—or even in the same picture. Former Democratic gubernatorial nominee John Jay Hooker, Jr., Democratic Congressman Harold Ford, Republican Congressman Robin Beard, Bill Brock when he was Republican National Chairman, and I at the barbecue in Memphis trying to help the "Keep Justice Brown" campaign.

In 1980 George H. Brown, Jr.—in the center—became the first black ever to serve on the Tennessee Supreme Court. I appointed him when Joe Henry died. The State Republican Executive Committee nominated him. I campaigned with him. Brown carried his hometown of Memphis and East Tennessee, but most Middle Tennessee Democrats would not support him and he lost. I later appointed him circuit judge in Memphis in 1983, and he was reelected.

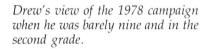

Drew's view of the 1978 campaign when he was barely nine and in the second grade.

Leslee's second grade prose at Ensworth School in 1980.

THE LIFE OF BEING THE GOVERNOR'S DAUGHTER

The first thing that happened was that my family and I almost traveled around the state with Daddy. After that there was the election. We waited a while at the Opryland Hotel and then we turned on the TV just in time to see who won. We were so happy that we won! My father made a bunch of speeches and we went right home and started packing.

Then we moved in on a Wednesday. A while after that my mom had a baby. It was the fourth one. His name is William Houston Alexander.

-Leslee Alexander
2nd Grade

First Place, Prose

Promoting Fan Fair, a great Nashville institution, with, among others, Mario Ferrari, T. G. Sheppard, Sheriff Fate Thomas, and William Golden of the Oak Ridge Boys.

Ode to Dissecting an Earthworm

Dissecting an earthworm, you'll never want to do it.
Trust me, really, you'll barely get through it.
The worm, you might think, would be mushy, I know.
It's not, it is hard and tough and so.
I know it sounds gross but its not all that bad.
But you'll have to do it, so try to be glad.

Kathryn Alexander
Grade 6

Kathryn's poem when she was eleven.

LBJ'S granddaughter is persuasive! This is Jennifer Robb—granddaughter of President Lyndon B. Johnson and daughter of Virginia Governor Chuck and Lynda Bird Robb—putting a hammerlock on Will Alexander at the 1982 Governors' Conference in Williamsburg. Jennifer and Will have become good friends, just as we have with the Robbs.

What I have enjoyed most, in specific: Visiting classrooms, watching great teachers inspire students.

What I have enjoyed most, in general: Setting the agenda and seeing things happen.

My riskiest decision: The early swearing in, January 17, 1979. Most Americans don't favor coups, which is what that was.

Most inspiring athletic performance by an Alexander: To Honey, who beat me in tennis on Sunday afternoon, May 13, 1979, and gave birth to Will the next morning.

The best kept secret in 1980 presidential politics: Howard Baker led the national Republican delegate hunt one to zero for a few minutes at the Arkansas convention.

The finest action by a public official while I was governor: By Lewis May, district attorney in Upper East Tennessee, when he asked me to pardon Douglas Forbes, a man he had mistakenly put in prison for rape.

Fortunately, the Japanese Ambassador Never Asked about the Silver Service on the Sideboard. It was the captain's silver, recovered from the U.S.S. *Tennessee*, which Japanese warplanes bombed at Pearl Harbor. The silver is in the State Dining Room at the Governor's Residence where we have entertained Japanese business executives and diplomats more than one hundred times.

Honey hates heights and doesn't really like sleeping outdoors, so, typically Honey, she joined an Outward Bound expedition for thirteen days and rappelled down cliffs in the North Carolina mountains.

Three of the hardest things I had to do as governor:

1. *Cutting the budget*—Raising taxes is a piece of cake compared to reducing the size of government, even during a recession.

2. *Emphasizing excellence when it costs money*—Chairs of Excellence, Centers of Excellence, Master Teachers, Governor's Schools for the Gifted, Bicentennial Parkways—all run against the grain: the natural impulse in government is to level, and leveling is the enemy of excellence.

3. *Declining Ron Harries's application for clemency*—It was an open and shut case. There was no basis for clemency. I support capital punishment in the worst cases. But it still is not easy to be the last person to make that decision.

The three events that surprised me by how much they touched me:

1. Hearing the first master teachers describe what the new Career Ladder opportunities meant to them at what was supposed to be a routine board of education meeting to approve their certification in 1985.

2. Playing the piano with the first student orchestra at the Governor's School for the Performing Arts in July 1985. I suddenly realized what it must mean to a French horn player from Chuckey and a flutist from Greenback to have this opportunity, and I remembered how the orchestra was only an idea five years earlier.

3. Offering the toast to President Reagan on behalf of the nation's governors at the end of a White House dinner in February 1986. I was struck by just how special the presidency is to the governors and to all Americans.

The biggest unsolved mystery: What is the meaning of the name of the Cherokee town, Tanasi, that gave our state its name?

Best fishing in Tennessee (and therefore the world): Go with Steve McAdams for crappie on Kentucky Lake near Paris, or with Bill Dance for bass around Memphis or sauger at Pickwick Lake in December, or with Gilbert Webb for trout at Abrams Creek or the middle prong of Little River in the Smokies.

Five Books That Made a Difference to Me

The best book on communicating: *Ogilvy on Advertising*, by David Ogilvy, especially his ten points on typography.

The funniest book: *Crackers*, by Roy Blount, Jr.

The book that changed my thinking the most during the last ten years: *A God Within*, by René Dubos.

The book that I read when something slows me down: *The Discoverers*, by Daniel Boorstin.

The book that every American family ought to read: *Roots*, by Alex Haley.

No wonder the news seems confusing. When "Today" visited the Knoxville World's Fair in 1982, Jane Pauley accompanied me on the washboard, and Bryant Gumble interviewed the world's greatest guitar player, Chet Atkins, about politics.

There may not be another application for admission to practice quite like this one in the archives of the Supreme Court of the United States.

CERTIFICATION

I certify that I have read the foregoing questions and have answered the same fully and ...kly. Said answers are complete and are true to my own knowledge.

<u>L awar Alexander</u>
(Signature of applicant)

...d this **21ˢᵗ** of **October**, 19**69**

STATEMENT OF SPONSORS

We, ... RICHARD NIXON .... and
(Print or type names in full)
...OWARD H. BAKER, JR. ...., being members of the bar of
...upreme Court of the United States and not related to the applicant, state that the applicant
...rsonally known to us, that ...**HE**... possesses all the qualifications required for admis-
(He or she)
...to the bar of the Supreme Court of the United States, that we have examined ...**HIS**...
(His or her)
...nal statement and believe it to be correct, and we affirm that ...**HIS**... personal and pro-
(His or her)
...nal character and standing are good.

(Signature) ....

(Business address) The White House

(Signature) ....

(Business address) U. S. Senate

...e were many different ideas ...t how to keep one's eye on the ...t Winfield Dunn's inauguration ...970.

"The Meeting at Blackberry Farm" became a buzzword in national political circles after several Republican governors and congressmen met there in July 1985, to plot strategies for winning more state and local offices. The lodge at the farm in Miller's Cove has been my favorite retreat for planning.

In this photograph, Gilbert Grosvenor, president of the National Geographic Society, Sheldon Coleman, whose company makes the famous camping lanterns, and Victor Ashe, executive director of the President's Commission on Americans Outdoors, discuss the commission's work during its session at the farm in 1986.

More Favorite Quotes

"I like Tennessee. At least they don't tax you every time you turn around." ED GAYLORD, Oklahoma City, owner of Opryland.

"The second bite of the apple is not as sweet." GOVERNOR BUFORD ELLINGTON, in 1970, when governor-elect Winfield Dunn asked how Ellington enjoyed his second term.

"John Jay Hooker? I thought he moved to Florida." WINFIELD DUNN, in 1975.

"The best way to raise the average is to improve the best." DESMOND HUDSON, president of Northern Telecom.

"You don't choose your words for what they mean; you choose them for how they taste." HOWARD BAKER to EVERETT DIRKSEN.

Recruiting Japanese industry: Someone has to do it.

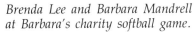

Brenda Lee and Barbara Mandrell at Barbara's charity softball game.

"Never stoop so low to hate," BARBARA (MRS. GEORGE) BUSH'S favorite quote from "Daddy" King (Dr. Martin Luther King, Sr.), whose son was assassinated, whose other son drowned, and whose wife was shot in the face and killed.

"The abuse doesn't mean a thing to me. I've been booed by twenty-four thousand people at once." DALE KELLEY, commissioner of transportation and former Southeastern Conference basketball official, after a two hour grilling by the House Transportation Committee.

"The governor of a state always comes first in protocol, ahead of the former president of the United States, the Queen of England, anybody but the then-president of the United States. I've had a terrible time getting governors to recognize that." DEAN RUSK, the former secretary of state at lunch at the Executive Residence.

"When Slats uses one of our trucks to put out a fire in Decherd, we charge him one week's sales tax collections at the Decherd Red Food Store." The mayor of Winchester, HOWARD HALL, walking with the mayor of Decherd, Slats Shelly, in a Homecoming parade, describing intergovernmental relations Tennessee-style.

"Some people say we Tennesseans live south of the Mason-Diction line." WILMA DYKEMAN, state historian, Newport.

"Communities, not governors, fix schools." DAVID MATHEWS, president of the Kettering Foundation, examining Tennessee's local Better Schools Task Forces.

"What we are trying to do is to get people to think big and to understand that common sense is common sense." BOB WATERMAN, co-author of *In Search of Excellence,* visiting in Nashville.

"Some people watch people on television not because they like them but because they're interesting or even because they dislike them." IRVING WAUGH, on why Floyd Kephart stayed on WSM television when so many people complained about him.

"Something like the idea of Homecoming is good because it helps us instill in the younger people the values of the older people before they die and pass on." REXINE PIGG, Hot Rock, Tenn.

"Well, slap the dog and spit in the fire." NAOMI JUDD, when she and daughter, Wynonna, won the Country Music Horizon Award in 1985.

"I Don't Have Time to See Her." "You'll be sorry if you don't," I told Ron Ziegler. In 1970 a Kentucky friend had asked me to help Diane Sawyer get a job in the White House. The friend had, if anything, underestimated how attractive and smart she was.

I didn't make many suggestions to Ron Ziegler. He had an *important* job as President Nixon's press secretary, and my job as Bryce Harlow's telephone answerer was at least three or four rungs down the ladder. But Ron took time to see Diane and hired her on the spot. Since then her ability has propelled her through the television news business to become the first woman broadcaster on "60 Minutes." She took time to say hello at the 1984 Republican Convention in Dallas.

What's Next?

"What's it like?" I asked Pete duPont, one year after he had finished eight years as governor of Delaware.

"It takes six months to quit waking up worrying about what went wrong yesterday," he replied. "It was August before I could enjoy the morning newspaper."

Another governor, running for the United States Senate, told me, "I have to keep running. Politics is a treadmill. If you get off, it's almost impossible to get back on."

Unlike Pete, who wants to be president of the United States, I've made no big decisions about what to do next. And unlike my other governor friend, I don't mind the risk of stepping off the political treadmill.

The Alexanders have made no big decisions, but here are some modest ones.

To Live in Australia for Six Months. After eight years in the Governor's Residence, we are ready to try living together more normally as a family for a while. And for a family everybody in Tennessee recognizes, Australia is a good place for us to try that. It's halfway around the world; it's great outdoors; it's summer there in January when my term ends; and we know no one. Then we'll settle in Tennessee. My heart will always be in Blount County where our home is in Miller's Cove; but we will live where I work.

To Write Two Books. The first will be about being governor, about lessons learned in the very best job in the U.S.A.; the other with my brother-in-law Bill Carl will be *A Preacher and a Politician.*

Not to Haunt the Next Governor. There can be only one at a time.

Not to Be a Professional Former Governor. I have nightmares of being presented as a relic at banquets and charity events, ball games and political rallies. Not for me.

To Help Howard Baker Be President If He Wants to Be. But as a citizen-friend, not as a campaign manager.

What appeals to me? To discover an idea as big and fun and worthwhile as the National Geographic Society or "A Prairie Home Companion" and help it happen. Garrison Keillor imagined "A Prairie Home Companion," the Minnesota public radio show that is America's latest cult, while visiting the Grand Ole Opry on a hot summer night. And one room in the National Geographic headquarters in Washington has a ceiling upon which the stars are fixed just as they shone on the night in 1888 when thirty scientists at the Cosmos Club organized the society.

Ideas are where you find them.

ing by Dana Fradon; © 1985   The New Yorker Magazine, Inc.

"On the one hand, I know I could make more money if I left public service for the private sector, but, on the other hand, I couldn't chop off heads."

KEEPING THE WAGON IN THE ROAD

Some days being governor is like hanging from a helicopter over a pit of hungry alligators, and there is a cheering crowd of onlookers around the pit who feel about the way the Romans felt about the Christians in the arena—my fall would be someone's idea of good entertainment. On other days the job is like coaxing a team of mules to pull a wagon in the direction they're *not* headed. On most days it is an accomplishment just to keep the wagon in the road.

To gain a head start on the alligators, I get up at 5:00 A.M. That gives me time to work in the pine-paneled study downstairs at the Residence and to run a couple of miles before I have breakfast with the family at 7:00. The rest of my day is supposed to follow a card that is sectioned for every fifteen minutes.

What really happens to my precisely programmed day is often different. Take June 25, 1985...

As I am preparing to leave for tomorrow's six-city tour to announce the results of the first Career Ladder teacher evaluations, a letter arrives from the attorney general saying the prisons are so overcrowded I'll probably have to commute the sentences of hundreds of prisoners. While I'm still chewing on that one, a press aide catches me and says that fifty-one pounds of uranium have been discovered buried at Oak Ridge. I delay my flight for two hours to talk with the attorney general and to find out whether the press aide meant pounds or tons.

Or, take the next Monday, July 1... About 2:00 P.M. I am planning the next meeting of the National Governors' Association when word arrives that propane trucks have overturned in Knoxville and that it could be as bad as the Waverly railroad explosion in 1977. Downtown Knoxville is being evacuated. The propane disaster is barely under control when I'm handed a radio report that St. Jude Children's Research Hospital in Memphis, one of the premier medical facilities in the country, has decided to move to St. Louis. I track down University of Tennessee President Ed Boling to talk about St. Jude (the UT medical units, I believe, are the key to keeping St. Jude in Memphis), but at 7:45, I am interrupted: there is a prison riot at the Turney Center—two hostages, three burning buildings, attack squads on the way. It is the new Corrections commissioner's first test.

And so it goes. Still I have used the schedule, despite all the interruptions, to try to focus on the activities that would move Tennessee ahead, leaving cabinet managers most of the job of keeping the wagon in the road. And I have learned to enjoy the rich diversity of each day as a governor.

The Second Best Cure for a Governor Who Gets Too Big for His Britches: staff meetings, every morning at 8:30, with a group of highly talented, loyal, and irreverent men and women, schooled in the tradition of the Walk Across Tennessee and absolutely dedicated to moving Tennessee ahead. (The *best* cure? Putting on the red and black shirt and getting out of the Capitol to visit with "real" people talking about "real" concerns.)

Staff meetings discourage memo writing, and I am convinced the less memo writing there is, the more good government there is. Too often, people who write memos are merely justifying their positions. Instead, we learned to rely completely on each other in fast-moving situations: "Did you tell the (legislative) leadership?" "Will it be done before 10:00 A.M.?" "Are you sure the law permits it?" "Can I arrive on time?" "What is the filing deadline?"

That's how our staff worked; that's the way we got results.

A Conversation at Our House around the Dinner Table Recalling the Vice President's Visit.

Father: Which friend is Caroline?

Kathryn: Caroline is the one who met George Bush with wet hair. Remember? You got all mad at us because we didn't have time to get ready.

Mother: You had time to get ready. You just stayed in your room listening to the radio and . . .

Leslee: See, Kathryn.

Drew: Go get her, Leslee!

Kathryn: Mommmmmmm!

Kathryn, left, and Caroline Hagan with George Bush.

Every Minute of Every Day can be spent trying to help start an academy for teachers of writing, recruit one more distinguished faculty member to a state university, create a new system of bicycle trails, or say "thank you" or "congratulations" or "I need your help" or "I'm sorry" to someone in Tennessee. A staff member took this photograph in Narita Airport in Tokyo in 1985 after I had finished my secret three-day trip to meet with Toyota officials. I was outlining Tennessee's proposal on a yellow pad before starting the fifteen-hour flight home.

But a tired governor is not a very creative one and certainly not a pleasant one. So I have tried to carve out time for rest and for the things our family enjoys. On Sundays there is no schedule except church. As often as possible, nothing was planned during the children's spring school break and on weekends. We've taken summer vacations, and I'm home most nights for supper and to bed by 9:00 P.M.

Tennessee's governor is commander in chief of the nation's finest National Guard units. Adjutant General Carl Wallace, right, and Robin Beard, then a congressman and now the top U.S. civilian at NATO and a marine colonel. In 1979 I spent the night in the barracks at summer guard camp in Mississippi and ran the four-mile early morning run with the troops.

Turkey and Dressing Looked Mighty Good After Eating Raw Tuna—especially when the tuna kept opening its mouth and flapping its tail. It usually was still alive after being cleaned and sectioned—and, for the most part, eaten. That's why the Tennesseans who had been living in Japan learning how to make trucks the Nissan way were so happy to have a real Tennessee Thanksgiving dinner in Tokyo in 1981. Honey joined them while I visited Taiwan.

Honey has learned to enjoy the freshness and color and simplicity of Japanese food. I am a more timid eater. Early on I learned to stir a little mess on my plate giving the impression that I had eaten something. More than once an ominous looking piece of squid or eel or unidentified raw meat found its way into my coat pocket. And I am still trying to learn to eat rice balls with chop sticks.

One of the more important prerogatives of the governor is to be able to walk at the front of Columbia's Mule Day parade, which is exactly where you want to be in a parade of mules . . . unless you are an especially high stepper.

I Always Walk in a Parade. What is natural about riding in an open convertible sitting on the top of the back seat waving at people who are not looking at you? Maybe if you're the homecoming queen, riding is a good idea. But for a politician whose job is to be close to the people, walking and shaking hands and talking to people along the way is the logical thing to do.

In case there is a Three Mile Island in Tennessee. The state's emergency operations center works hard and well on emergencies of all kinds, which means the center is busy almost every day. We've not had a nuclear accident, but in case one ever occurs, we will know what to do because of regular drills such as this one.

Was It Nuclear War, the Prison Conditions, or the Truckers on Strike Again? The Nashville Symphony and I were halfway through Paderewski's "Minuet in G" when two people began running through the crowd unfurling a banner. I had wondered whether it would be possible for a governor to play an open-air concert in Centennial Park before five thousand people without an interruption.

The large crowd had pushed the front row nearly onto the stage. Someone in the second row had already suffered a seizure, and after the ambulance arrived, the paramedics fought their way to the patient, who was just in front of me. I kept playing. The television cameramen, anxious to record each wrong note, tried every angle including one just above the strings with the camera shoved six inches from my face. I kept playing.

During a country ballad, I lost my place and the orchestra raced ahead, about four measures ahead of me. I kept watching the maestro, Michael Charry, and we finished at approximately the same time, which was my goal. The protesters turned out to be two unpredictable friends, Tish Hooker and Huell Howser, and the Sunday afternoon concert was so much fun that I have performed with Tennessee symphonies and community orchestras twenty-seven times since.

I've never pretended to be a concert pianist, and it has not escaped me that I never was asked to perform with any symphony orchestra until I was elected. Vladimir Horowitz is older and better, but I am more available for a concert with the Greeneville Community Orchestra. Although I play the piano better than most governors, most of the crowd comes to count my mistakes!

It's Nice Living, But It's Not Home

"It's so sad," whispered my dinner partner as the young waiter poured coffee. "The prisoners these days are so much younger and seem so *nice*."

"The waiters are college students from MTSU," I assured her. "The prisoners went back to the main prison the day we moved into the Governor's Residence."

Prisoners began working at the Residence in 1953 shortly after the Clements became the first large family to live in the mansion on Curtiswood Lane. When Lucille Clement moved in with three children under eight, she found a woodstove in the kitchen, almost no furniture, a constant swarm of tourists, staff, state guests, and highway patrolmen...and no help.

A dozen or so "outside" prisoners were brought in to keep up the ten-acre grounds when they were not washing cars for the governor's friends or playing basketball at the hoop by the garage. A dozen "inside" prisoners cleaned the fifteen-thousand square foot house and cooked and served meals. Sometimes they served breakfast in bed. Other times they played cards in the basement.

When I visited Governor Blanton after my election in November, 1978, the prisoners served an African egg dish for breakfast. Halfway through the meal Blanton ordered all the "inside" prisoners to stand along the wall of the family dining room.

"Tell him your name, what you did, and how long you're here for," the governor said.

One by one, they repeated their names, their crimes—ranging from rape to murder, usually murder—and the lengths of their sentences, usually life or ninety-nine years. "They like to do it," Blanton said, grinning.

Betty Dunn worried about the presence of prisoners around the young Dunn children, especially after she found a prisoner's marijuana in a closet. Betty Blanton grew tired of having the prisoners always under foot. But it was hard to imagine how to run the busy mansion without the prisoners; taxpayers would surely squeal about paying to hire enough people to keep the first family in such perceived fine style. The Residence staff no longer includes twenty-four prisoners. Now, seven staff members help keep the grounds, plan the menus, and clean the house. Last year 13,000 meals were served at state dinners, policy breakfasts, and special events.

Most of the visitors to the Residence are Tennesseans, the real owners of the house—one of the nicest first-family homes in America. One woman spent two hours inspecting every thread downstairs and then wearily announced, "Now, where do they cook? I'm ready to see the kitchen!" While dressing upstairs I have heard the volunteer docents answer the questions of children who visit.

"Is the mommy here when the children come home from school?"
"Almost always."
"Who helps with their homework?"
"I'm not sure, but I'll bet it's mommy."
"Are the children here now?"
"No."
"Can we go upstairs and see their rooms?"
"No."

Honey has opened the house to the public on Tuesday and Thursday and at other times to public groups—like the women of Westminster Church or Leadership Knoxville. In 1986 thousands of visitors will come to the Residence.

The more visitors there are, the more state troopers on security detail there must be. Even as late as the 1950's, during the Clement years, neighborhood children played Red Rover on the front lawn. Now that there is a fence around the grounds, visitors must have a conversation with a loudspeaker at the front gate. That has made it possible for the troopers, who once sat at a desk in the front hall, to move to the basement, giving the family a little more privacy.

Sometimes the governor's staff meets at the Residence. Governor Clement often arrived in the early afternoon with several staff members, and a fair amount of state business was conducted around a pool table in the downstairs sunroom.

Sometimes there are official visitors. When presidential candidate Ronald Reagan and Mrs. Reagan spent the night in May 1980, Ed Meese—now the United States attorney general—slept in Will's bedroom, and Will moved in with us. We call the guest bedroom where the Reagans and President Ford and George Bush all have stayed the "Elizabeth Taylor Room," because—of all our famous overnight guests—she caused the most consternation among the house staff. Alex Haley runs a close second.

The "Elizabeth Taylor Room"

The State Drawing Room

Near the Elizabeth Taylor Room, Honey and her assistant, Carole Martin, have an office where the dozens of phone calls and letters Honey receives each week are handled. In the next room, where we keep our washer and dryer, a secretary answers the Residence phone and handles clerical work for the complicated Residence operation.

The melee can confuse the children of the first families.

"I've decided what I want to be when I grow up," young Bob Clement announced.

"What's that?" asked his father, the governor.

"A prisoner," said Bob. "They have the most fun."

The Residence is worth every penny it costs the taxpayers for one reason: it is the governor's best place to convene people. The most important Japanese executive in the early stages of the Nissan decision was Masahiko Zaitsu. In 1979 and 1980 he was a guest at the Residence eleven times—so often that the children began to think of him as some sort of Japanese uncle and he began to give tours to other Nissan executives who were visiting for the first time. My first dinner with Bill Hoglund, the president of Saturn, was at the Residence, just the two of us. When we want to present the Governor's Awards for the Arts or to honor the St. Jude

You Never Know Who Might Be Coming in the Sun Room Door. This parade of children of staff and cabinet members came to see us at Easter 1986.

The Greeneville Room

Children's Research Hospital Board for staying in Memphis or the founders of the 13–30 Corporation for staying in Knoxville, there is no better place than the Residence. Busy people stop what they are doing to accept an invitation to the Governor's Residence, and a governor who can stop busy people and head them in a direction that benefits the entire state is a governor who is doing his job.

My favorite places in this beautiful house are the pine-paneled downstairs study where I work early in the morning and the outdoor portico where we eat meals in the spring and summer, looking over the huge front lawn. At other times we eat together in a family dining room full of rare East Tennessee furniture donated by citizens from Greeneville. The most occupied place is

"What's at the top of those stairs?"
That's what most school groups ask
when they visit the Governor's Res-
idence. They also ask, "Who cooks?"
"Who helps with homework?"
"Whose horse is outside in the sta-
ble?" The horse is Leslee's and so
is this third grade class with Leslee,
third from the left in the first row.

our master bedroom, one of the five rooms in the huge house that are exclusively ours. The whole family and young guests retreat there at the end of the day. Sometimes it seems as busy as the entrance hall downstairs.

But, grand as it is, living in the Governor's Residence is more like living in a museum than in a home, and not too long after moving in, we began to miss our old home. More often than not on weekends we have rushed to East Tennessee—each of our children bringing a friend most times—and built dams in the streams, taught the children to drive in the pastures, or sat on the back porch looking at the open meadows and mountains with no iron fence in sight. Honey runs on Miller's Cove Road and cooks big Sunday breakfasts. We watch for bluebirds and deer and grouse on our hikes with Will up Hurricane Branch to the cow graveyard.

When we sold our home in Nashville we bought half a duplex at Hilton Head, where the only governor most people recognize is the governor of South Carolina and where we can ride bikes and walk on beaches without being noticed. If security could have been maintained and we could have afforded it, the one thing we would have done differently is to keep our home in Nashville and spend a lot of time there.

e Master Bedroom

TRYING TO DO IT RIGHT

"**They Never Understand. The Democrats Believe We're Up Here Plotting and Scheming and Trying To Do Them In,**" Jim Henry once said to me. He has had the double duty of being the Republican party state chairman and the Republican leader in the House. Some people think he is also a magician because with about one-third of the votes in the legislature he and Senate Republican leaders Tom Garland and Ben Atchley have been able to persuade the legislature to pass virtually every important proposal I have recommended.

"All we do," Jim continued, "is try to decide what the right thing is and then propose it as loud as we can and push it as hard as we can. When we do that, they've got no choice. Either they join us in doing the right thing, come up with something even better, or pay the political price at the next election."

The most successful people I've met in public life—in business or politics—spend most of their time figuring out what the right thing to do is and then doing it.

In March of 1985 I met briefly at National Airport in Washington with Roger Smith, chairman of General Motors. Tennessee badly wanted GM's Saturn plant. General Motors badly wanted Tennessee to pass a seat belt law.

"I understand you're within two or three votes of passing the seat belt bill," Roger said.

"I believe in it and I'm doing everything I can," I replied. "Does our passing the bill make any difference in the Saturn decision?"

"I can't honestly say it does," Roger said. "We want the seat belt bill, but the Saturn decision stands on its own."

If his answer had been yes, I might have found a few more votes for the bill. But the chairman of the world's largest company was careful to tell me the truth, even though the seat belt law—that year—failed to pass.

My best political ethics teacher was Bryce Harlow, for whom I worked in the Nixon White House in 1969 and 1970. Mr. Harlow had been President Eisenhower's favorite staff member, and he was Mr. Nixon's first staff appointment. For several months my desk was in the same room as Mr. Harlow's in the West Wing of the White House, not forty feet from the President's Oval Office. While handling his messages, I watched a steady parade of Nixon administration staff and cabinet members come to Harlow for advice.

One senior staff member was about to make a phone call to speed up a decision in a Federal Trade Commission case on behalf of one of the president's friends. "Do you remember why Sherman Adams resigned?" Mr. Harlow asked him. Adams had been President Eisenhower's chief of staff.

"Not exactly," said the staff member.

"It was because he made a little telephone call to the Federal Trade Commission to inquire about the status of a case for an old friend, who had just happened to give him a Christmas present the year before."

"That was all?"

"That was it."

The staff member dropped his phone call. Sometimes experience helps you know the right thing to do.

Once Mr. Harlow was looking forward to taking a week's vacation at an old friend's vacation home. Then, the friend called and asked for a small favor. Mr. Harlow waited a day or two before calling his friend back to say that the White House schedule had changed, and he wouldn't be able to take the long-awaited vacation trip.

"You will find," Harlow told me after that, "that the people you are least able to help when you are in public office are the people you know the best."

Why I Still Can't Eat at Ruby Tuesday's. I haven't eaten there, although it's one of the best restaurants in town, since Jake Butcher ran a 1978 campaign commercial accusing me of selling whiskey in the basement of a Gatlinburg church.

The facts were these: Honey and I owned 16 percent of a restaurant company, Ruby Tuesday, Inc., we were sure would become very successful under the leadership of our friend, Sandy Beall. Ruby Tuesday's Gatlinburg restaurant bought a nonprofit club charter from a church and then sold liquor-by-the-drink to its patrons in Gatlinburg. It was completely legal but it was hard to explain, especially since the governor appoints the members of the state Alcoholic Beverage Commission, which regulates such things. There were four weeks left in the campaign. Jake and I were neck and neck. I wanted to be governor more than I wanted to be rich, so we sold the stock for sixty thousand dollars. A year later the same stock was worth more than one million dollars.

Money—even little bits of money—can get politicians in trouble quicker than anything except lies. Honey bought a few shares, less than one percent of the stock, of Corrections Corporation of America. But she sold it when CCA changed its mind and decided it might try to do business with the state of Tennessee.

One Sunday in 1986, the *Tennessean* ran this front page headline:

"State Road Seven Miles from Governor's House." State roads were to be improved within seven miles of the houses of most people in the state, but the inference for several hundred thousand readers was that I was building a road to benefit myself. That same day I cancelled the road project, leaving the next governor to decide whether the public needs it. My action shouldn't delay the project, which is not scheduled to begin until 1991.

I have tried hard, and fortunately, Honey has been willing to cooperate, to do whatever it took to avoid the suspicion that, as governor, I was serving my own interest and not the public's interest. In 1974 I disclosed the names of all of my contributors and what they had given me. In Tennessee, no one had ever done that before. I have released our tax returns and net worth every year for the last eight years and have gone into painful detail with reporters when it was necessary. None of this is required by law.

A good many people think I overreact to situations like the *Tennessean* road story. Maybe I do. But I couldn't have much respect for anyone else who would let the capitol city's largest newspaper raise a question about his integrity on the front page and not do *something* about it. I've never complained about stories about my *policies*, even when the stories were wrong. This is a part of the price we pay for having a free press. But a politician's reputation for integrity is his stock in trade. That is why I cancelled the road, why Honey sold her CCA stock, why I have disclosed our tax returns every year, and why I still can't eat at Ruby Tuesday's.

"You Give the Same Answers, or You Can't Run the Show," Carol Marin, then a television reporter in Knoxville, told me after the tape didn't work on an interview she had agreed to conduct for

This is a photograph of Carol Marin, Nashville Banner *publisher Irby Simpkins, and* Chicago Tribune *editor Jim Squires talking about the incident at the Journalists Homecoming Reunion in 1986 at the Residence.*

my 1974 campaign. "My integrity is at stake," she said. "I'm not going to let you give better answers to my same questions the second time around."

During the second interview, she asked the same—or tougher—questions; I gave the same—or worse—answers, and she let me use the show. Carol is now a Chicago television personality and frequently appears on the "Today Show" when Jane Pauley is not there.

"Who's on the Flagpole?" In my first cabinet meetings I would say, "Why don't we do *X*?" Everyone would agree, "Let's all do *X*." A month later, *X* wasn't done. I learned the hard way that everybody does nothing.

I developed a new procedure. When something was important, some *one* went "up the flagpole." For example, I remember saying, "We need fifty-one votes for the bill to reorganize all the technical institutes, community colleges, and vocational schools and put them under the board of regents so we can deliver better job training for adults. Granville Hinton, you're on the flagpole." There was a big laugh, but everyone, especially Granville, knew that if we came up one vote short, it was his fault. Of course, we all would pitch in to help. But we knew, on that issue, Granville was in charge.

That may seem harsh, but it usually has meant that we've had a few votes to spare. Granny, by the way, got seventy-five votes for that bill. Otherwise, he would have have been flapping at the top of the tallest flagpole on Capitol Hill.

Eight of the first twenty-two cabinet members in my administration had been chief executives of private businesses, and they were especially impressed with the caliber and hard work of the professional state employees. Tennessee has never had better leaders and managers in the cabinet positions than it has had during the last eight years. Past and present cabinet members, plus some of my long-term staffers, assembled at the Residence in May 1986.

Women's firsts—the first two women state trial court judges, the first state party chairwoman, and seven of the first fourteen women cabinet members in Tennessee history. All Republicans, all appointed between 1979 and 1986, they are, left to right: Rose Cantrell, Ann Tuck, Sammie Lynn Puett, Marguerite Sallee, Susan Richardson-Williams, Julia Gibbons, Martha Olsen, Linda Rendtorff, Kathy Celauro, and Susan Simons.

The Last Leadership Meeting, April 30, 1986.

Governor Alexander: We've done this at 7:30 every Wednesday morning when the legislature was in session for the last eight years. When we look back on it, I think we will be surprised how important these meetings were. I know that they have been crucial to all the important things that have happened to help move Tennessee ahead during the last several years.

I don't know in how many other states a Republican governor sits down every week with the Democratic and Republican legislative leaders and discusses issues the way we have. We haven't made decisions for the legislature, but we certainly have set the parameters and constructed the environment for whatever good has happened here. Without sounding too stuffy, I simply want to thank you for that.

Speaker Ned McWherter: There is one thing we can say for sure— not once in eight years, never, has anyone used anything said in one of these meetings in a political speech from the back of a pickup truck to embarrass one of us. I've been to meetings of Speakers of the House from all over the South. Some of the speakers don't have any connection at all with the executive in their state, and usually they're all of one party.

Lieutenant Governor John Wilder: In some states, the *Speakers* don't talk to each other.

McWherter: I don't know if they do it in other states, either, but I know that here it has been very important.

Wilder: This is the way to do things. Some people think it's smart politics to act mad and never talk to each other. That's the way some people do it. But these meetings have been good. They have been good for the state.

One day at a Leadership Meeting Finance Commissioner Don Jackson, a new cabinet member, sat in Speaker McWherter's chair, almost causing the budget to be defeated. After the first few meetings, each leader had adopted a chair. And, somehow, the cosmos wasn't in order unless everyone was there and in his chair.

The composition of the group was a recipe for failure: the Democratic leaders were all from West Tennessee, the Republicans from East; the governor represented the executive branch, and the others represented a very independent legislature; one of them was the Republican state chairman, and one was the leading Democratic candidate for governor. There were huge arguments, but it all worked, and most of the talk in every meeting was devoted to figuring out the right things to do for the state of Tennessee.

On Twisting Arms. Sometimes I have seen as many as thirty or forty key legislators in the governor's office, one by one, just before a crucial vote. Here is how my end of a typical conversation went: "Charlie, I understand your responsibility to make your own decision on the seat belt bill, and if you decide to oppose it, I will respect that. But I wanted to let you know how it looks from my perch.

"I believe that if we don't pass the seat belt law it will cost Tennessee hundreds of lives and thousands of jobs. Our highway patrolmen tell me how many people they see with their heads stuffed through broken windshields.

"We were the first state to pass a child restraint law. And you know how much it has cut down on the deaths of children.

"I know that some people think it's a freedom question. But I look at seat belts like one more safety regulation, like driving on the right side of the road, like using your lights at night, like not driving while drinking and not speeding.

"And there's one more thing. American car companies won't be able to compete with imported cars if the federal government makes them add $820 airbags because we refused to pass the seat belt law. We need a hospitable environment for new automobile jobs in Tennessee and this will help.

"Your constituents will respect you if you do what you think is right. I think this is right.

"Now having said all of that, I really appreciate your letting me put my two bits in, and I'll end where I started: we need your vote; it will be close; but I will respect your decision no matter what it is."

I never was comfortable coming down much harder than that (although the staff and cabinet sometimes did), and I never traded for votes. But I never needed to, because this approach almost always worked.

Sam Houston Would Have Gone Ahead and Choked Him. One morning without warning, Lieutenant Governor Wilder excused himself from Leadership Meeting in order to vote for a bill that would have repealed the Career Ladder for teachers—a bill I was dead set against. The vote failed. Earl Warren, the state photographer, happened to be taking official photographs of the leadership that morning while Wilder and I discussed his vote in front of a portrait of former Tennessee Governor Houston.

John Wilder knows how to take political pressure in stride. Once in a Leadership Meeting, he told us about an especially thorny issue he was going to have to decide. "And the biggest lobbyist for

the bill is a preacher. The preacher told me that he had talked with the Lord and the Lord wants me to vote for the bill. I told the preacher that I had a good relationship with the Lord, too, and that if He wants me to vote for it, the Lord should speak to me directly."

Three Tough Questions

1. *"Why do you want to be governor?"* Honey encouraged me not to run again in 1978 unless I could tell people why I wanted to be governor. It is a surprisingly hard question. The candidate who answers it best usually wins. At the Gridiron Dinner in Washington in March 1986, Senator Ted Kennedy told a story about television broadcaster Roger Mudd.

"There he was," the senator said, "my friend of twenty years . . . sitting in *my* chair . . . in *my* yard . . . by *my* swimming pool . . . taking up *my* time . . . drinking *my* drinks . . . and asking me trick questions like: 'Why do you want to be president?'"

Kennedy did such a terrible job answering that question on Mudd's nationally televised interview that he withdrew from the 1980 presidential race before it started.

2. An even trickier question is, *"What does a governor do?"* I finally developed my answer after reading George Reedy's *Twilight of the Presidency* in 1978—John Seigenthaler gave me the book right after I was elected—and have stuck with it for eight years:

A governor's job is to:
• see the state's few most urgent needs,
• develop strategies to address them, and
• persuade at least half the people that he or she is right.
That's it.

3. *"How does a governor do it?"* For years I have tried to find the best way to explain how a governor does best what a governor ought to do. The image I like to use is that of Count Basie. Basie was a bandleader whose mere presence at the piano helped bring out the very best in whatever group of musicians was assembled. The best examples of that in Tennessee today are Tennessee Homecoming '86 and the Better Schools program, two movements bringing out the best in hundreds of Tennessee communities.

One Reason You Have Governors

"One reason you have governors," Governor Bruce Babbitt of Arizona once told me, "is to make exceptions when they need to be made."

I thought about Bruce's comment when I looked at my schedule card for May 15, 1985: "3:15—3:30, meeting with Jim Word, re: Courtney Parham." The case of the Memphis two-year-old was sandwiched between meetings with legislators on the seat belt bill and the taping of a Governor's Report on nursing home regulations.

Jim, who was commissioner of the Department of Health and Environment, and I were meeting because of a letter I had received from Courtney's mother. At birth, Courtney's spinal cord had been stretched and her neck broken in a forceps-assisted delivery.

"She was fortunate that her brain was not damaged. She has the normal intelligence of any child her age," her mother, Cindy, had written me on April 12. "Courtney's life is totally dependent on a respirator connected to a tube in her throat. The tube becomes disconnected no less than ten times a day. When that happens, she becomes unable to make a sound and within a few short minutes she will be gone if she does not have constant twenty-four-hour supervision by registered nurses."

The state would have paid to take care of Courtney in an institution, but Cindy Parham wanted her daughter at home. "Because the only thing she can move is facial muscles, her face comes alive when she talks. She loves her family like any child and does not like to be separated from us for even short periods. We understand that you alone have the power to create and grant a waiver that will allow us to keep our daughter at home."

Cindy's letter was one of 150 that arrived in my office on April 16. As usual, the Department of Health and Environment had drafted an answer for me to consider. My meeting with Commissioner Word was scheduled because I didn't like the answer. It said there were no funds to take care of Courtney at home.

Senator Al Gore had written asking that "Courtney not be allowed to fall through the cracks." A Mississippi TV newsman had quoted one Washington official as saying the matter was up to the state of Tennessee and the state of Tennessee simply didn't care about Courtney.

Jim Word had caught the brunt of this. His job was to find ways to keep Medicaid spending under control. The program had grown from zero to six hundred million dollars in fifteen years, and the legislature, just the day before, had approved our proposal to freeze benefit levels. That meant more money for better schools and a balanced budget. But it also meant no help for Courtney.

"Cookie, my wife, told me that I won't be able to stand this very much longer unless I find a way to deal with this problem," Jim said. "I'm a bleeding heart liberal when it comes to helping people. I think I've found a way to help Courtney. I'm going to Memphis in the morning to see her family. If you will give me some budget flexibility, I think there is a way to do it."

"Jim," I said, "you go to Memphis tomorrow. We'll *have* to find a way to help her and people like her. Call me when you come back." I left to tape my radio spots.

Later that afternoon, on the way to the Governor's Residence, I received a message on the car radio to call Lewis Lavine, my chief of staff.

"I'm afraid it's not been one of our best days," Lewis told me when I reached him. "The seat belt bill failed fifty-seven to forty. And Courtney Parham died at 3:05 this afternoon, just minutes before your meeting with Jim Word began."

FRIENDS– MOSTLY NEW

"**I feel like Alice in Boogertown.** You know we lived in Boogertown a while, for a couple of years." It was May 1986, the opening day of Dollywood in Pigeon Forge, and Dolly Parton and her guests were touring the museum depicting her life. We came to a picture from the Washington trip for the 1963 Sevier County High School senior class. "Where are you?" I asked. "There, in the front row, in the center. What did you expect?" she said laughing.

Dolly got the idea for Dollywood "about 1980 when I saw that big neon sign up above those Hollywood Hills and thought about sneaking up there one night and swapping a D for the H and seeing how long it took anybody to find out. But I had been dreaming about having a place like this, to give something back to where I grew up, ever since I went out on my own about 1974," she said. "This is the happiest day of my life, even though I was sucking bugs every five minutes (because of the outdoor lights) at the concert last night!"

Neil Diamond sent one thousand balloons to Dollywood for opening day. Other celebrities had wanted to come. "I hope I didn't hurt their feelings by not wanting them here, but I wanted it to be just for me."

I'm not sure what difference it would have made if other celebrities had come. People would have still been looking at Dolly. I've been around a lot of celebrities, but only around two that people just want to stare at. The other one was Elizabeth Taylor. In 1980, at a fund-raising dinner in Nashville, grown men—presidents of banks and businesses—would come up to the head table where Elizabeth was sitting beside me and say "Hello, Governor," and then literally spend three or four minutes just staring at her. I had never seen anything like it, that is, until I spent some time with Dolly at the opening of Dollywood.

"Would you please get out of the way, Governor, so we can see her?" "Hey, Dolly," everybody shouted as we rode through the crowd in a 1909 Lewis roadster.

"I'm sure a lot of those people are out here just to see you, Governor," Dolly said, trying to make me feel a little better. I didn't mind. I was looking at Dolly, too.

"I Ain't Never Heered Nothing on You—Yet." On Thanksgiving weekend of 1983, I sat on Lem Ownby's bed. He sat in a chair by the Warm Morning stove, which was busy taking the bite out of the cold air that had followed us into the cabin where he lived by himself. As we talked, the smell of Blood Hound chewing tobacco and wood smoke gradually replaced the freshness of the frosty air. Lem was ninety-four and blind, and when he stood he was not as tall as Honey. Fifty years earlier, when the Great Smoky Mountains National Park was created, the park service let Lem stay at his cabin on Jake's Creek, with the beehives, snakes, and bears he had grown up with.

"We haven't had many governors from East Tennessee," I observed. Lem answered quickly: "Yeah, and we ain't had many that didn't steal either." Then, with a laugh, he said nothing bad on me had gotten to Jake's Creek—yet.

"I'm a Republican all right," he said without my asking. "You see that corner?" He pointed to a corner of the cabin by the unused fireplace. "My mother was praying right there for her seven brothers to come home from the Civil War when they all walked into the yard. She was still on her knees. They were all Union soldiers."

Lem died in the freezing cold later that winter.

Two Years after this 1982 "Firing Line" Appearance I Sat Next to William F. Buckley at Dinner, a $1 million Howard Baker fund-raising roast in Washington, D.C. Buckley was the master of ceremonies.

"When do you write?" I asked him.

"Anytime," he replied. "Books are about the only thing I write in a methodical way. I do them in Switzerland, after I ski, between about 5:30 and 7:00 P.M."

I told him that when our family had visited Chartwell, Winston Churchill's former secretary said that Churchill sometimes dictated 5,000 words in a night.

Buckley was surprised. "I can do 1,100 or so in a couple of hours," he said. "Sometimes more, maybe up to 2,800 words at a time, but 5,000 would be a very productive night. With the advent of computer technology I can know exactly what I do each time I write. For example, my last book took 112 hours."

"When do you make corrections?"

"I do that in about thirty minutes the next morning, before I go skiing."

"You mean that you finish off the last day's work so you can be ready to start when you return from skiing?"

"That's right. Then I send the transcript to five friends. When the transcripts come back, I put the five edited versions side by side and decide what changes to make."

The best advice I ever received from the third grade. Mrs. Schwepfinger's Room, Walnut Hill School, Harriman

If I Were Governor

If I were Governor of Tennessee, I would have the streets cleaned up with a third of the tax money. Then I would take a fourth of the tax money and try to stop acid rain. I would take another part of the taxes and pay the teachers better. After I did all those things I would probably feel drowsy so I would go to sleep. After I woke up I would use the rest of the taxes and make banks and railroads safer places. After there was more tax money I would clean up toxic wastes.

Bobby Bradshaw
3rd Grade
Mrs. Schwepfinger's Room

"What about your columns? How long do they take to write?"

"You mean after I get them in mind?"

"Yes."

"About twenty to thirty minutes. Westbrook Pegler once told me it took him eleven hours to do a column."

"Do you make changes?"

"No. I've been doing it for nineteen, no, twenty-two years. I know the rhythm, the internal consistency of the column. I have it down. I don't change it. That would be like asking a jazz pianist to change his improvisation."

"The Governor Got Two Judges for the Price of One That Day." That's what George H. Brown, Sr., told friends after he raised his hand, too, when George, Jr., was sworn in. What would *you* have done if your son was about to become the first black Supreme Court Justice in Tennessee's history, you were standing next to him, and the clerk said "George H. Brown, please raise your right hand and repeat after me"?

George, Sr., was a car cleaner on the Illinois Central Railroad. Sometimes he tried his hand as a "jackleg lawyer" to help workers who got into trouble. He helped put his sister through college, but when she was ready to teach and to help him through college, he had a growing family and went instead into the military.

"If he could have picked a professional career, he would have been a lawyer," George, Jr., says of his father. "He's shrewd and he loves talking and arguing. He's as independent and bullheaded as I am. You're talking about a black guy growing up in the Depression when he couldn't have *named* two or three governors, let alone help elect one who his son calls by first name. You cut through a whole lot of history and society there."

I had some great teachers, but Miss Lennis Tedford was the best. From age five until my high school senior recital, I spent thirty minutes with her each week, and because of that, got up at six every day to practice for an hour (well, almost an hour) so my afternoons would be free for things I *really* wanted to do.

"Don't play that monkey business," she would say. She could always tell when I'd been playing too much Jerry Lee Lewis. "I can tell you've been doing it by the way your left hand is jumping."

From Miss Tedford I learned more than music. She taught me the discipline of Czerny and the metronome, the logic of Bach, the clean joy of Mozart. She encouraged me to let my emotions run with Chopin and Rachmaninoff. She made sure that I was ready for the annual piano competitions and that I performed completely under control.

In 1981, when I played with the Maryville Community Orchestra, Dr. Bob Haralson pushed Miss Lennis's wheelchair down front in the middle aisle. I gave her thank you flowers. I know that she squirmed a little each time I missed a note.

A Visit with H. Ross Perot

On September 28, 1984, I flew to Dallas to visit H. Ross Perot at his billion dollar computer company, Electronic Data Services.

Perot had been making the papers. He was third or fourth on *Forbes* magazine's list of America's richest persons. The day before he had purchased a copy of the Magna Charta for $1.5 million.

About two thousand people work at the EDS complex, close to downtown Dallas. It has swimming pools and a nine-hole golf course for the employees. As you walk through the door into Perot's office, there is a sign on the right: "Every good and excellent thing stands moment by moment on the razor's edge of danger and must be fought for."

We began our twenty-five-minute meeting at 9:45. Perot is small, probably about five feet six inches or five feet seven inches. His nose reminds me of mine, which caught a softball one time. His eyes are bright. He is straight to the point, easy to talk to, and listens well. I was there so we could compare the Texas and Tennessee school reform movements, both of which had just worked their way through tumultuous legislative sessions.

Some topics Perot discussed:

• *Running for governor of Texas:* "Nelson Rockefeller told me, 'Your grandson will have fun, but people who make money can't run for public office.'"

• *Selling EDS to General Motors:* "We will be the automation advisor to General Motors. General Motors is like a small country. Maybe in twenty-five years we will be as big as GM is today. It's like giving a civil engineer a chance to build a bridge across the San Francisco Bay and to rebuild the Brooklyn Bridge and two pyramids if he has time."

• *Money:* "Money is not important to me. I have made so much that the amount is an abstract figure. I can't eat it. What is important is twenty-five years of work and opportunity for our employees. For twenty years I've made a point to provide them with work and never let them be laid off."

• *School reform:* "It has been the meanest, bloodiest, and most difficult thing I've ever been into. I've spent one hundred percent of my time on it in Texas for a year. My job is done. I don't think the people in Austin want to see me again for a while. . . . People have been to see me about how to do what we've done in their states. I tell them, unless you can get the governor involved, don't even start. It will be a waste of your time."

• *Lobbyists:* "I was amazed at the power of the lobbyists. One of the best things about a special session of the legislature is that the lobbyists aren't working. I hired the best ones. If you hire the right ones they can pass an anti-gravity law."

120

"Scape-Goto"—That's what the two dozen American governors who were competing for the Nissan plant called Mitsuya Goto, because it would be his job to come back around to tell the governors who *didn't* get it.

One Sunday afternoon in Yokohama we visited Goto's home, a rare privilege in Japan where homes are more private than in the United States. Goto swapped stories with John Parish, a Tullahoma businessman who is about the same age and was then chief of Tennessee's Economic Development Department.

"I was a boy in Nagoya during World War II," Goto said. "When the American fire bombers flew over, the other boys hid, but I ran into the streets. The fires were so bright and the planes flew so low I could see the pilots' faces. Then I would go back inside my home and carve tiny replicas of the war planes I had seen."

I had visited Nagoya. Because of the heavy bombing during the war, the city has no trees more than forty years old.

About the same time that Goto was watching the bombers flying above Nagoya, John Parish had been pushing his nose against the chain link fence around William Northern Air Force Base in Tullahoma. Every night the search lights lit the sky while B–29's dropped sand bags on practice targets. *Had they been some of the same B–29's,* John wondered, *that flew to Nagoya?*

"I have a present for you, John," Goto said and rushed upstairs. He returned with two perfectly carved miniature war planes, replicas of the planes he had seen nearly forty years ago.

Today John displays those planes in his Tullahoma home at the edge of the runway at William Northern Air Force Base. They are two of his most prized gifts from one of his best new friends.

"You Know, He Really Liked You Even If You Are a Republican." I had stopped by Miss Maybelle's front row seat to pay my respects at the October 1981 funeral of her husband, Robert N. Clement. The sound of her greeting broke a respectful silence. Her words reverberated through the Dickson First Methodist Church sanctuary like the bass notes of the pipe organ. They rolled and bounced along the pews upon which sat four hundred of the state's most prominent Democrats, squeezed shoulder-to-shoulder.

"Miss Maybelle always speaks a little loudly because she's hard of hearing," her daughter, Miss Anna Belle, whispered to me.

"Don't apologize," I whispered back. "Four hundred Democrats heard everything she said."

I liked Mr. Robert too, even though he was a Democrat.

My political life has been strangely tied up with the Clements. When Mr. Robert's son, Frank Clement, told four hundred and fifty of us at Boys State in 1957 that "one of you boys is going to grow up to be the real governor of Tennessee," I thought he meant me. He was the first governor I'd ever met. Later, I voted for him in the Democratic primary in 1962, causing my Republican father nearly to have a stroke (not because of Governor Clement, but because I was voting in the *wrong* primary). Then, in 1966, I helped Howard Baker beat Governor Clement when both wanted to be U.S. Senator.

In 1981, when it came time to select a chairman for the legislature's reform task force that led to our better schools movement, the speakers and I chose Anna Belle, Frank's sister. She then ran for governor in 1982 when I was running for re-election. A year and a half later she provided the decisive vote to pass the Better Schools Program after her nephew, Frank Clement, Jr., headed up the bipartisan citizens group for educational reform, Tennesseans for Better Schools.

When Bob Clement, Frank's other son and now the president of Cumberland University, presented me with an honorary degree in May 1986, I reminded him how much the Clements had contributed to Tennessee political life for thirty years.

"It's true that my dad once suggested that Lamar ought to run for governor one day," Bob told the commencement crowd, "but what Lamar forgot is that Dad meant that he should run as a Democrat!"

Here Come the Baseball Cards! For an eleven-year-old boy— our son Drew—meeting George Steinbrenner meant the promise of a stack of baseball cards. And, to Drew's delight, within two weeks the cards arrived, revealing George to be a man of his word.

When the Nashville Sounds were affiliated with the Yankees, Steinbrenner gave us good players and winning teams. We've had season tickets on the front row ever since opening day of the first Sounds season.

"I Can Track an Ant Across the Sahara Desert in a Wind Storm with My Eyes Closed!" Those were the last words I heard Dwight McCarter say as I went to sleep by a campfire near Cades Cove. Dwight is a mantracker, a Smoky Mountain back-country ranger. If you're lost in the Smokies, he's the one they'll probably send to look for you. And if you stop he'll find you. He says most people who are lost get in trouble when they keep running, following a creek, looking for a way out, which is what I remember my Boy Scout manuals said to do if I was lost.

Walking along through the mountains, Dwight will see and hear a hundred things that you will miss: boar droppings, bear claw marks high up on a tree marking the edge of a bear's territory, grouse ("if one flies out, there's usually another one left"), trailing arbutus, daffodils where old home sites used to be, and ruts in the creek beds cut by the steel wagon wheels as they bumped down Rabbit Creek trying to avoid the tangle of the rhododendron thickets, which the pioneers called "hells."

One Sunday afternoon I found Dwight on Chilhowee Mountain dusting old beech trees with chalk. He had spent the day copying messages that mountain men left a century earlier. "They knew these big, old beech trees would be here a long time. I figure that carving on them was the only way they had of making a mark in life back then," he said.

Senator Baker Had Just Told the President a Joke about John Hinckley and Moammar Khadafy, If You Can Imagine That. Not all presidents laugh so easily. When I attended a Ned McWherter dinner in Dresden in December 1982, the head table was full of people who had tried hard to keep me from being governor, including Jimmy Carter. "President Carter must like me," I told the audience. "He comes up to Tennessee every time I run."

When it came Carter's turn he recognized me last. "I've done about as much to help Lamar Alexander as he has done to help me," he said. His smile was as big as ever, but it seemed frozen, and he was testy. "And," Carter continued, "I believe the record will show that I have carried Weakley County every time I have run, and he hasn't." I was surprised he took my joking so seriously.

In contrast, President Reagan always seems to be in genuinely good humor. When Honey sat next to the president at the White House dinner for governors in 1986, which was held the same night that President Marcos was being ushered out of office with obvious U.S. encouragement, President Reagan told a steady stream

of funny stories until he was interrupted by a waiter with a telephone message.

"I can't tell you what that was. It's a secret," President Reagan told Honey. A second message arrived an hour later. The president said, "Well, I can tell you now, the first message was wrong. Marcos has not resigned." And his stories continued.

They Poured Coffee down His Back When He Sat at the Lunch Counter.

"Who did that?"

"White people," Pete Drew will tell you. "I took it. I had to take it then because I was committed to nonviolence. But I was a fighter, a boxer. And after a while I decided not to take it anymore. God was good to me, though; He looked out after me, and I got out of all of that without any bad scars."

Pete was in Augusta, in Birmingham, in Nashville, in Virginia, and in Maryland, wherever the action was in the civil rights movement in the sixties. He was not an important leader then. Today he is.

After trying twice to be elected to the Knoxville City Council, he was elected to the county commission, then to the legislature as a Democrat in 1982. He switched to the Republican party in 1985 when he was vice-chairman of the Legislative Black Caucus. He still is a fighter and still strongly religious. He is the kind of black Republican the Republican party must attract to create a two-party South.

Why Do the Alexanders Wear Seat Belts? When "Bubba" Gay was assigned to security duty at the Residence, he was one of son Will's favorite highway patrolmen. Bubba was twenty-two and newly married. At staff parties, he could beat staff chief Tom Ingram at tennis—and Tom is a superb player. Early one April Sunday morning in 1981, as Bubba was driving home from his all-night shift at the Residence, a car traveling more than one hundred miles per hour knocked his car through the intersection at Nolensville Road and Harding Place. When Drew and I returned that night from fishing in Abrams Creek, we went straight to Vanderbilt Hospital. There was not much hope that Bubba would use his legs again, and he never has. How he survived at all is a miracle.

Will already rode in a child restraint seat, but Bubba's accident has caused the rest of us to think often about wearing seat belts. We also think often of Bubba.

I Do Not Know Her Name. I watched her bright face from the moment we entered the fourth grade mathematics class at Vishnevya School No. 3 on the outskirts of Kiev. She and her thirty classmates stood erect in uniforms by the side of their desks. Her desk was in the front row.

Most Soviets, even most Soviet children, do not have such a bright and happy face. As we were leaving, Honey asked the class, "Do you like school?" The girl with the bright face in the front row answered before anyone else could, and in perfect English, "Yes, very much!" just as I took this snapshot.

Four out of five students at School No. 3 study English; the rest study Spanish. They also speak Russian and Ukrainian. Two thousand seven hundred children attend this school in two shifts from 6:00 A.M. to 6:00 P.M. for 204 days each year (compared to our 180). The building was only six years old but the combination of so much use and poor construction made it seem much older.

Everyone is exposed to constant propaganda. In the history classroom a phonograph recording of a World War II Russian general recounted the horrors of Stalingrad. Some students wore red arm bands, "something to do with party duty," we were told. One part of the building was dedicated to the "participants of the Slovak uprising." Slogans and war pictures were plastered everywhere. There were one hundred forty teachers, seventeen of whom were Communist party members, including the harassed but pleasant principal (called a director). Some of the best teachers were paid more than others.

This beautiful child in the mathematics classroom in School No. 3 stays in my mind. Will she ever have the chance to learn and decide for herself what is happening in the world? That is the main difference between the Soviets and us. We learned, for example, at Kiev University that the Soviet people are told that the United States—not the Russians—shot down South Korean airliner 007 on its way to Tokyo.

In May 1986, when the nuclear reactor outside Kiev melted, I thought about her—and the lack of accurate information about almost anything in the Soviet Union—again. *Is she safe? Did anyone even tell her family about the dangers of the accident before it was too late?*

"What's It Like Having Minnie Pearl As a Next Door Neighbor?" Humbling, for one thing. The second Sunday after I was sworn in, Honey and I were standing on the patio of the Governor's Residence looking down toward Curtiswood Lane. Tour buses were coming by every few minutes and slowing down.

"How nice. The tourists are slowing down to see us," I said.

"Slowing down," Honey corrected me, "in front of the Governor's Residence so they can stop in front of Minnie Pearl's house next door."

It's also handy to have Minnie for a neighbor. She lets us use her lawn to park cars when our visitors overflow. And she's a crafty tennis partner. (Husband Henry calls her best shot the "Pearl Drop.")

Most of all, she's just plain fun. At her seventieth birthday party at the Governor's Residence in 1982, I played the piano and Roy Acuff led the "Happy Birthday" singing. Roy told her, "You're too old to cut the mustard, Minnie. You might as well cut the cake."

"Boy, I'm glad they didn't put all the candles on that cake," said Minnie, who has been known to capture the center stage pretty quickly. "It would be the biggest fire since Seth Jones' barn burned down! You know the fire engine in Grinder's Switch is named after me . . . because it's always ready and seldom called." Two hundred of her closest friends—including Chet Atkins, Pat Boone, Tammy Wynette, Del Wood, Grandpa Jones, and Ralph Emery—laughed harder than ever at jokes they had heard many times. Minnie is *always* better than ever.

The chance to live next door to Minnie Pearl is reason enough to run for governor of Tennessee.

YESTERDAY'S VALUES TOMORROW'S JOBS

"If the spider web is still here when the first Saturn rolls off the line, you will have done your job." I offered that challenge to Saturn President Bill Hoglund on the day Saturn landed in Maury County. State photographer Earl Warren took the photograph just after dawn a week before the announcement. Earl also discovered some Spring Hill ladies who had been getting up in the early morning for several weeks to take photographs of Spring Hill as their Homecoming project. They were planning to keep the pictures as a souvenir of what "Spring Hill was really like in 1986," long before they ever imagined that the world's largest new investment was coming to their town of eleven hundred.

Almost every top Saturn executive has a copy of the spider web picture hanging in his or her office as a reminder of their company's commitment to help Tennessee keep yesterday's values while we're getting tomorrow's jobs. Saturn has painted the picket fence around its property white, kept the old Haynes Haven home, plans to let horses graze on the grass, and is even worrying about choosing the best color for the plant buildings.

The word has gotten around ... Tennessee is a special place to live and work.

The Nissan decision in 1980—in the midst of a national recession that hurt Tennessee more than most states—was the watershed. After a six-year search, the meticulous Japanese had found the best place in the United States to make the largest overseas Japanese investment ever. And it was to be made in a state that had never had an automobile plant. Heads turned. Other Japanese companies followed. By the beginning of 1985, 10 percent of all Japanese capital investment in the United States was in one state: Tennessee—an inland state with only three thousand citizens of Japanese ancestry.

The most important photograph in Tennessee's future. This U.S. Defense Department satellite photograph of the United States was taken at night. Look where the lights are, then look where Tennessee is—in the center of most of the lights. Two-thirds of all Americans live within five hundred miles of our borders.

Then in 1984 a New York state university's survey put Knoxville—the city that travel writer John Gunther had called in 1947 "the ugliest city in America"—at the top of the list of the "Best Places to Live" in America. Distinguished scientists began to accept joint faculty appointments at UT–Knoxville and the Oak Ridge National Laboratory in an area atomic scientist David Lilienthal once told colleagues was an "intellectual wasteland." Rand McNally also put Knoxville, Nashville, Johnson City, Kingsport, and Bristol high on its list of best places to live. Chattanooga raised more money for the arts than any other city its size in the United States. In 1984 *Money* magazine said Cookeville and Crossville were among America's best places to retire. In 1985 *Runner* magazine named Johnson City the number one running city in America. As the airline industry deregulated, Northwest, by 1986, operated 156 flights a day out of its Memphis hub, and American put over 100 flights a day into its new Nashville hub.

Some of the companies that had known our state the best looked for greener pastures but decided to stay at home. Alcoa and Eastman invested several hundred million dollars each at their sixty-year-old plants in East Tennessee. Holiday Corporation built a new headquarters in Memphis. St. Jude Children's Research Hospital stayed in Memphis, despite a tempting offer from Washington University in St. Louis. And 13-30 Corporation chose to expand the headquarters for its national publications in Knoxville instead of

Connecticut. Meanwhile, other homegrown companies of all sizes were prospering. Federal Express added two thousand jobs in 1984 in Memphis. Hospital Corporation of America in Nashville created a new $2 billion joint venture with Equitable of New York, and most of the headquarters operations are coming to Tennessee.

TVA predicts Tennessee's economy will grow faster between now and the year 2000 than that of any other state in its region. A North Carolina banker told me his computer graphs keep showing Tennessee "breaking out of the pack," moving ahead of the rest of the states in the South. The U.S. Department of Commerce says Tennessee will be the tenth fastest growing state between now and 1990. New capital investment in Tennessee which was $400 million a year in the 1970's was *$4.5 billion* in 1985. And the most important statistic of all, the level of family income, which was 50 percent of the national average during the Depression and ranked Tennessee forty-fifth among all states in 1979, had moved up to fortieth in 1985.

Saturn president Bill Hoglund's first Nashville press conference in 1985 was the icing on the cake. A crowd of out-of-state reporters demanded to know why General Motors was putting a $3.5 billion investment in Tennessee when other states had offered a billion dollars if GM would come there. "That's not what we were looking for," Hoglund said. "We wanted the best place to build the highest quality car at the lowest cost so we could compete with the Japanese. We liked Tennessee's location and work environment. And we liked Tennessee's commitment to excellence in education, especially to paying more for teaching well. That's our philosophy, too."

"Your Wife Saved My Child's Life. I want you to thank her for me," a young woman in Alamo, Tennessee, said.

"What do you mean?" I asked.

"Prenatal health care," the woman answered. "Your wife told us

131

about it and brought it to us. Without it my baby wouldn't be alive today."

Honey's Healthy Children Initiative, funded generously by the legislature, has pushed health care for pregnant women into every county, tried to find a medical "home" for every newborn child from a poor family, and improved our ability to help babies in high-risk circumstances. As a result, fewer babies are born mentally retarded. And fewer babies die in Tennessee today than ever before. Think what that means for our future.

Two or Three Times I Was Sure This Call Was Going to the Governor of Georgia, but Nissan President Marvin Runyon called at 11:30 on Thursday morning, October 30, 1980: "Lamar, we're coming to Tennessee."

The first time I had met Marvin—two months earlier for lunch at the Governor's Residence—I was sure all was lost. Marvin was in a foul mood. A Nashville hotel had lost his suitcase—for the third time—and he let me know right away that he was a *close* friend of Governor George Busbee of Georgia, our closest competitor for the plant. Then he began to discuss concessions that we could not make, ones which I thought we had settled already with the Japanese. Marvin is now a good friend and great community leader; but when he left after lunch that day, I was ready to call Busbee and congratulate him.

Earlier that year we had found at Smyrna the only Tennessee site Nissan would accept, but the land owner, Maymee Cantrell, wouldn't sell. I flew to Maymee's home in Waverly one February morning. She served me sweet iced tea and her specialty, key lime pie. "Maymee," I said, "I hope you will let Nissan buy your land. It will tell the whole world that Tennessee is the best place to do business and bring jobs to people who need them."

"I don't want to sell," she said, "but I believe in what you're trying to do. The problem is our caretaker, Mr. Ward. I promised him he could live on the farm, and I won't break my promise." We helped Maymee find Mr. Ward a new farm ten miles away, and she sold.

But Maymee's 437 acres weren't enough. Nissan wanted the McClary's 260-acre farm too. Mr. and Mrs. McClary were in their seventies, and the farm had been in Mrs. McClary's family for one hundred years. We talked it over on a hot June night, rocking on their screened porch. They also agreed to sell.

In 1983, when the first Nissan truck rolled off the line, I saw Mrs. McClary as we both left the jubilant ceremony.

"How do you feel?" I asked her.

"We did the right thing for the people of the area," she said. "I know that. But if you really want to know the truth, I can't say it makes me happy to lose our farm."

"You Don't Suppose There's Anything to This Saturn Stuff, Do You?" That's what Peter Jenkins asked me early in June 1985. He called while I was spending a week in Hilton Head, working on my book about Japan and Tennessee. "I guess there's about a ten percent chance that speculation is right," I told Peter. "But the ten percent is a strong ten percent."

I then explained why. I had seen Roger Smith, the General Motors chairman, at dinner a few days earlier and had kidded him about conducting his nationwide search just to get a lot of publicity for his new Saturn car.

"Oh, no," he told me. "We locate several new car plants every year, and that's not the way we do it."

"How *do* you do it, then?" I asked.

"We send our people out without anyone knowing it to look over the community. If they don't already know, they live there and find out what the community is like, what the people think, and what it would be like to live there. We decide where we want to go, we option the land, and most people will read about it in the newspaper after the land is already optioned."

Peter didn't wait long to respond. "Well," he said, "the newspaper today says that General Motors has optioned twenty-seven hundred acres of land in Spring Hill, about half a mile from our farm."

I Wrote This Ad, Then Spent Almost All of the State's Annual Advertising Budget on It. For $450,000 the state of Tennessee bought a ride on the largest advertising blitz in automotive history. General Motors had not spent a penny advertising Saturn, but the intense competition for the Saturn plant made the front pages for months in 1985. As a result, twice as many people can identify a Saturn as can identify a Pontiac, even though Pontiac has been building cars since 1926 and Saturns won't be produced until 1990. The ad answered the question that was on everybody's mind for a few days in August 1985: "Why Spring Hill, Tennessee?" It gave us a rare chance to tell the Tennessee story and ask companies planning new investments the big question: "Saturn is here. Nissan is here. Where are you?"

Eric Ericson's ad agency put the ad together and placed it. During the National Governors' Association meeting in Idaho, the ad began a ten-day run in most national papers. I saw the power of the Saturn story when Honey and I went to a Mitch Miller concert in Sand Point, Idaho, later that week and he mentioned Saturn twice. I decided to spend the rest of the advertising budget by running the ads in Tennessee papers. Some legislators thought it was a waste of money, but if we don't know and believe in what Tennessee has to sell, who out of state will believe?

I Was Ready to Resign in 1984 If the Better Schools Program Did Not Pass. My idea was that Lieutenant Governor John Wilder would serve as governor, and I would run in a special election in November 1984 and put the issues straight to the people: Shouldn't we pay teachers more for teaching well? Is it tolerable for one-third of the eighth graders in Tennessee not to know eighth-grade skills? Will you pay higher taxes for excellence? Was I right to veto teacher pay raises just for more of the same?

I wanted to take the battle away from the legislative chambers where the lobbyists for the teachers' union were fighting my reforms tooth and nail. I asked Brad Reed, who had served as my campaign lawyer, to research the question and tell no one. Brad only asked, "Are you serious?" "Dead serious," I told him.

He returned in a week. "You can't do it. You can't serve three consecutive terms." So I continued the fight in the legislature.

No one doubts there is better teaching and learning in Tennessee schools today than there was before the program passed. But the Better Schools Program's biggest dividend for Tennessee families is better jobs. Our school reforms—especially the Career Ladder—have become the symbol of a willingness of Tennesseans to go pioneering again, to be first, to be among the best, to set high standards, and to achieve them. If the Tennessee Education Association is able to repeal the reforms they will also repeal most of the new public support of public education in Tennessee and much of Tennessee's new-found reputation as one of America's most progressive and admired states.

"THE BOTTOM LINE"

OUR SCHOOL CHILDREN

DANiel

THE KNOXVILLE JOURNAL

Tennessee Has Jumped to Third in Tomato Production. Tomatoes are grown in Tennessee for the same reason that cars are manufactured here: central location. It costs more to ship a tomato from California back East than it does to grow it. So we've put new money into tomato research, and we are encouraging a rebirth of the fruit and vegetable industry in Tennessee. Growing such crops means a second or third income for many families who need it. This could be one reason why in 1984 there was actually an increase in the number of farms in Tennessee from ninety-seven thousand to ninety-eight thousand.

TVA Flooded Part of Hawkins County for Sissy Spacek, and in return the makers of *The River* spent $8 million in Hawkins and Sullivan Counties and donated part of their location site as a park. I've been surprised to find that so many Hollywood personalities with Tennessee connections—Danny Thomas, Dinah Shore, David Keith, Huell Howser, Alex Haley (when he lived there), Delbert Mann, Jerry Reed, and Dorothy Ritter—all still have their hearts in Tennessee, and they have helped us persuade producers to make movies in Tennessee. Almost entirely because of good recruiting, our movie business has gone from $14 million in 1979 to $169 million in 1984, making Tennessee the fourth most important movie-making state. "No state has a better film commission," famed producer Bernard Schwartz told me when he was making *Sweet Dreams* here.

My On-the-Job Education

During the first two years I was governor, these facts made me stop and think:

1. The average family income in Tennessee was 81 percent of the national average, forty-fifth among the fifty states.
2. One-third of our eighth graders did not know eighth-grade skills.
3. Our high school dropout rate was 28 percent, fourth highest in the country.
4. Twenty-five percent of our college freshmen did not know basic reading, writing, and computing skills even though they had a high school diploma.
5. Only 11.5 percent of Tennessee adults had a college degree (before you jump out of your skin, the national average is only 14.5 percent).
6. No Tennessee public university was listed among *New York Times* Education Editor Edward B. Fiske's "291 Colleges You Are Most Likely to Attend"; three North Carolina public universities were listed.
7. Not one state paid one teacher one penny more for teaching well.
8. Freshmen in the College of Education at the University of Tennessee–Knoxville had the lowest entering academic averages of students on any of the thirteen campus colleges.

Education Exam   name *Lamar Alexander*

Essay Question: Explain how education can improve to better prepare our children for the future.

I would instigate a "Better Schools Program," the cornerstone of which would be establishing a system of "Master Teachers." Under this plan there would be merit pay raises for teachers who demonstrate outstanding ability. They would be evaluated by a committee of

9. Tennessee teachers, on the average, were about as well paid as the taxpayers who paid their salaries.
10. One-fourth of the graduating students of the Memphis public schools—75 percent black—were on welfare within a year after they graduated.
11. Tennessee's infant mortality rate was twelfth highest in the country.
12. Twenty-seven percent of Tennesseans' jobs were in manufacturing, more than in most states.
13. Japan had 10 percent of the world's money and would have to make in the United States much more of what it sold in the United States.
14. Sixty percent of all the people in the world lived in countries that border the Pacific Ocean.
15. New investment in Tennessee during the seventies averaged about $470 million each year, importing about twenty-one thousand new jobs each year.
16. But about two hundred thousand Tennesseans needed new jobs every year because nine thousand Tennessee businesses failed every year.
17. And about ten thousand to eleven thousand new businesses were created in Tennessee every year (when the economy was good).

Then I learned that . . .

18. Because so many Americans move to southern and western states like Florida and Texas, Tennessee has moved to the geographic center of the bulk of the United States population.
19. Transportation costs are the costs most businesses can do something about; they are 20 percent of the Gross National Product.
20. Businessmen were saying that the pro-jobs environment and the right-to-work law in Tennessee were their main reasons for locating or expanding here.
21. No state in the center of the United States market north of Tennessee has a right-to-work law.
22. Manufacturers want good roads even more as they adopt the idea of just-in-time delivery of supplies.
23. Large manufacturers prefer industrial sites within an hour's drive of attractive large cities, not more than ten miles from an interstate highway, and as near as possible to railroads.
24. Three thousand Ph.D.'s live and work in the Oak Ridge/Knoxville area.
25. Most school buildings are closed half a year.
26. About one-third of Tennessee parents can have some choice of public schools for their children if they ask for it.
27. There are a lot of potentially fine teachers of all ages who have a college degree but who don't want to spend four more years in a college of education.
28. Nearly two-thirds of all Tennesseans live in six urban areas, but most of us still have our roots in three thousand smaller places with names that Tennesseans proudly call home.

On This I Sound Like a Broken Record

The preceding facts and the following conclusions may help you understand why I say time and time again that paying more for teaching well should be Tennessee's most important strategy:

1. Tennessee's most urgent need is to raise family incomes.
2. Higher family incomes come from jobs, not from government handouts.
3. Most new jobs are grown at home, not recruited.
4. "Growing" and holding jobs today requires higher skills than many Tennesseans have.
5. Skills are usually learned in schools.
6. *Therefore, better schools mean better jobs for Tennesseans, young and old.*
7. The teacher-student relationship is the heart of a school.
8. *Therefore, better teachers produce better schools.*
9. Many talented people will not join a profession that does not reward performance and results.
10. Taxpayers will not pay teachers' salaries that average much above their own (taxpayers') salaries.
11. Taxpayers *will* pay to make Tennessee's best teachers among the best-paid teachers in America because the taxpayers' jobs depend on the teachers' results.
12. *Therefore, paying more for teaching well is the best way to keep and attract the best teachers.*

Raising family incomes is much more complicated than what I have just outlined; but basing policy on this series of conclusions for ten years will do more than anything else the state can do to raise family incomes.

Courtesy of *The Knoxville Journal*

One Governor's Report Card

As my term draws to a close, people often ask, "What are your accomplishments?" I know what they are thinking. Saturn and Nissan came, so I must have talked Saturn and Nissan into it; the schools are better because of *my* Better Schools Program; there are new roads—the governor built them; fewer babies die—Honey's programs saved them. Some think about it the other way, too. Prisoners escape; I must have gone to sleep at the watchtower.

But that is not the way it is, and that is not the way I mark my own report card. *Governors* don't have those kinds of accomplishments; *the people* do. A governor achieves his personal best by being honest and by staying in touch with the people who elected him to serve them.

A Tennessee Report Card (1979–1987)

Here is my list—in priority order—of the twenty-five most important things that state government helped happen during the last eight years (aside from the birth of William Houston Alexander, May 14, 1979). Most of the twenty-five things are programs and policies based upon the facts and conclusions you have just read:

1. MASTER TEACHERS AND PRINCIPALS—Tennessee, five years ahead of the nation in paying more for teaching and leading schools well, offering 77 percent pay increases over three years to the best teachers with twelve-month contracts.

2. TENNESSEE HOMECOMING '86—Seven hundred ninety-

eight communities, studying their heritage, thinking prouder and bigger, all at once, in one state, the biggest celebration in our history. (If we could bottle the spirit, it would outsell anything else in Tennessee!)

3. SATURN AND NISSAN—The biggest United States investment ever and the biggest overseas Japanese investment ever both coming to Tennessee, a national verdict about where to build the highest quality car or truck at the lowest possible cost in the 1990s.

4. NEARLY 10 PERCENT OF ALL JAPANESE UNITED STATES INVESTMENT COMES TO TENNESSEE—Developing the best relationship any state has with America's number one ally.

5. THREE BIG ROAD PROGRAMS IN SIX YEARS—More than doubling the gasoline tax to build one of the best state road systems, including 152 miles of new state-paid interstate highways.

6. KNOXVILLE'S OAK RIDGE CORRIDOR—Building an interstate highway from the nation's most visited national park (Great Smokies) by the airport for the most livable city in the U.S. (Knoxville) to the world's finest energy research laboratory (Oak Ridge), giving joint appointments to twenty-five nationally distinguished scientists at the laboratory and at an improved UT–Knoxville, building a $25 million technical institute on the corridor, all in an area where 3,000 Ph.D.'s live and work, creating Tennessee's answer to North Carolina's Research Triangle.

7. CENTERS OF EXCELLENCE AND CHAIRS OF EXCELLENCE AND ONE HUNDRED PERCENT FUNDING FOR HIGHER EDUCATION—Endowing our colleges and universities so they can do better what they do best.

8. THE LOWEST INFANT MORTALITY RATE IN TENNESSEE HISTORY—Fewer babies die, because there is the Healthy Children Initiative. (Honey would put this first. She's probably right—she almost always is.)

9. CLEAN WATER PROGRAM—Safe Growth Team's most important accomplishment: $1 billion of government money over twenty years so there will be enough safe water.

10. BETTER SCHOOLS TASK FORCES—One hundred twenty-five local citizen groups setting *their own* goals and issuing *their own* report cards, because ultimately communities fix schools.

11. BASIC SKILLS FIRST—New standards and tests so we can insist that eighth graders know eighth-grade skills.

12. COMPUTER SKILLS NEXT—Computers and training so that every ninth grader knows basic computer skills.

13. ELIMINATE MOST CEILINGS ON INTEREST—They were running away money and jobs.

14. SCENIC PARKWAYS SYSTEM—No new billboards or junkyards on three thousand miles of roads to scenic places (unless cities and counties change their zoning).

15. GOVERNOR'S SCHOOLS—Four month-long residential Governor's Schools for gifted high school juniors in the Sciences, Performing Arts, Humanities, and International Studies; a Governor's Academy for Teachers of Writing; Principals' Academies, plus

several hundred Levels II and III teachers teaching summer classes for other students who want to get ahead and students who need to catch up.

16. STATE PRISON OVERCROWDING PERMANENTLY ENDED—New corrections laws put state prisons in best shape in a long time. (I'm sure the Democrats will wince at this. It's always been on their gripe list.)

17. REORGANIZED ADULT JOB TRAINING UNDER BOARD OF REGENTS—To help adults who need basic skills, computer skills, and new jobs skills.

18. COLLEGE FRESHMEN WHO NEED THEM MUST TAKE REMEDIAL COURSES—Twenty percent need them, even though they have a high school degree.

19. PRIVATE MANAGEMENT OF CORRECTIONS—More pioneering to see if someone else does it better for less money.

20. ABOLISHING MEMPHIS STATE UNIVERSITY'S UNDER-GRADUATE TEACHER EDUCATION PROGRAM—In its place is a master's degree program attracting talented men and women who already have college degrees in their teaching fields and who want to be teachers. It's the wave of the future.

21. TENNESSEE HERITAGE OF MUSIC—Three million dollars in endowment and annual operating funds for symphonies and community orchestras.

22. MEMPHIS JOBS CONFERENCE—The catalyst that helped our largest city find its strengths, celebrate them, and move ahead.

23. TENNE-SENIOR— Retail discounts for 530,000 Tennesseans sixty-five and over.

24. TOURISM BECOMES A $4 BILLION INDUSTRY—With the help of Tennessee Homecoming '86, a big advertising budget, and the World's Fair.

25. ALL DONE WITH THE LOWEST TAXES IN THE SOUTH—State and local per capita taxes in Tennessee are the lowest in the South; there are a thousand fewer state employees than there were eight years ago, the state debt has been reduced six of the last eight years, and Tennessee is one of eleven states with a Triple A bond rating.

Honorable Mention:

Clean Roadsides—A litter pick-up crew in every county.

Medical Home for Every Child—So every poor child has a doctor.

Tennessee Tomorrow—So tomorrow's political leaders can meet today's.

Jobs for High School Graduates—Skills and jobs for high school graduates who otherwise would have been *least* likely to succeed.

"Just Say No"—Preventive measures to halt the alcohol and drug epidemic among young Tennesseans.

I figure everyone else will develop a report card for the last eight years so I might as well offer my version.

Very Few of These Twenty-Five Actions Would Have Happened If I Had Not Learned That a Good Name Helps to Persuade At Least Half the People You're Right. Whoever named the "Right-to-Work Law" guaranteed its success. Whoever named the "Monitored Retrievable Storage System" (MRS) helped to guarantee its failure. Opponents labeled it a nuclear dump before the rest of us found out it is only a place to repackage used nuclear fuel before it is sent out West.

The importance of putting a plain English name on a policy or program is a hard lesson for professional and government people to learn. The president asked me to chair the Outdoor Recreation Resources Review Commission. I agreed but renamed it the President's Commission on Americans Outdoors. Once I was asked to speak on "school/college articulation." I spoke instead on "What Colleges Expect High School Graduates to Know," which is the same thing. Our legislators changed the name of the "Better Schools Program," which causes taxpayers to rise spontaneously from their chairs to cheer public education, to "Comprehensive Education Reform Act," which induces sleep before the fourth word. They turned "Master Teachers" into "Career Level III Teachers."

In 1982 I put the state's most urgent needs into a corporate mission statement that everyone could understand:

> Our job is to help to create safe, strong, and clean communities where children can grow up healthy, receive a first-rate education, and find a good job.

Most of my time as governor has been spent achieving goals related to this mission, even at the expense of other important state functions. Our policies, strategies, and programs carried out this mission. And a lot of time went into giving the strategies and programs names that developed popular support for their enactment and eventual success.

On a rainy afternoon you might try to match each of the twenty-five most important actions to one part of the corporate mission. For example, "Strong Communities: Tennessee Heritage of Music." They all fit.

SOUNDING LIKE WHERE YOU GREW UP

"When you stop sounding like where you grew up is when you start getting into trouble."
—Roy Blount, Jr.

We became very good, in the third grade, at smashing snowballs into the windshields of Ohio cars that were racing toward the Florida sun. We had a safe spot and a short throw from behind the Blount County fire hall at the end of Ruth Street in Maryville. Nothing was more exciting than watching a speeding Ford full of sour-looking Yankees—sour, we assumed, just at the *thought* of having to slow down in a place like Maryville—slide sideways to a stop on icy Highway 411 and roll down the windows all at once and shout in the direction of the fire hall, "You blasted little hillbillies. Go home to your mothers. Stop throwing those snowballs at our cars."

In my hometown, we didn't worry if Ohio tourists called us hillbillies. In fact, we celebrated it. The first time I ever saw Minnie Pearl, Smiley Burnett, Francis the Talking Mule, and Pat Boone all at once was at the 1956 Hillbilly Homecoming in Maryville. And by the third grade, our East Tennessee attitudes, tastes, and sounds were forever formed. We climbed in the Smoky Mountains most weekends, belly laughed at Homer and Jethro's bad jokes ("She tried to wear mama's girdle but she didn't have the guts"), and learned to eat right (fried ham, fried chicken, fried okra, boiled potatoes, wilted salad, hot pie, corn bread in buttermilk, and beans).

There were occasional concerts by Dame Myra Hess and even Vladimir Horowitz, but what stirred us most was joining hands at the Rankin family reunion and, swaying in concert with eyes directed toward the rafters, mournfully singing "Blest be-eee the tie-eye that binds," which was written by a Rankin ancestor in 1858.

The best snowball thrower in Maryville is in the center of the second row.

Most of all, we *sounded* like hillbillies. A real East Tennessean's "i's" are as flat as river rocks when he says, "It's a right bright night for a nice knife fight." This manner of speech, like most of a person's other most important characteristics, is something you can't learn—or get rid of—after about the third grade. You've heard Tennesseans who try too hard to unflatten their "i's." It sounds awkward and funny and everyone suspects something's wrong with them.

While I never worried about the Ohio tourists who seemed to look down on the Tennessee way of life, I began to notice that other Tennesseans did worry. For example, when I was in college the television program "College Bowl" wanted the University of Tennessee audience to wear overalls: the UT students instead put on tuxedos. Memphis has argued for years about changing the name of Mud Island, which is just right because that is what it is, to Volunteer Park, which is just wrong because that name has nothing to do with Memphis. I invited Charlie McCoy and his country band to play at the Governor's Residence the first time Saturn executives came to Nashville. One Nashville woman was embarrassed that I didn't arrange for Chopin preludes instead. Why offer average Chopin when you've got the greatest harmonica player in the world?

When Saturn President Bill Hoglund made his crucial private visit before the Saturn decision, we fed him fried okra, corn on the cob, biscuits, and country ham for dinner. I worried about it at 3:00 A.M. when I woke up thirsty from the ham, because I figured he was waking up, too, and he wouldn't know why. But if he had wanted veal piccata he could have found that in Michigan or New York. He was looking for a different environment for Saturn, so he came to Tennessee. And one of the first things he did was buy some country hams from Early's Market outside Spring Hill.

About once a day I encourage Tennesseans to follow Chet Atkins's advice: "In this life you have to be mighty careful where you aim because you might get there." But people who spend time

trying to take the mud out of Mud Island or to unflatten their
"i's" don't have much time left to focus their aims. In other words,
most of the help I have tried to give community by community can
be broken down into five words: *Be yourself, then think bigger.*

In Tennessee, this advice is easier to follow these days because
some things have changed. Instead of Mel Tillis singing about
busloads of hillbillies leaving Tennessee for jobs in "Detroit City,"
Detroiters are signing up to work at car plants in Tennessee. "The
sons and daughters of our cousins are coming home" is the way
Peggy O'Neal Peden put it in Peter Jenkins' calendar for Tennessee
Homecoming '86. Tourists in the Ohio cars that once sped through
town are now stopping to buy tickets at Opryland and Graceland
and to camp in the Smokies. Some of the people who used to
laugh at us are moving here. They like it because we've held on to
some values other places have lost.

Tennessee Homecoming '86 helps make certain we chart a steady
course during this welcome turn of events. It reminds us to sound
like where we grew up. It's good advice the world over. The most
popular Australian these days is Dave Hogan who appears on
American television commercials that begin "G'day" (pronounced
guh-die). What has made Hogan popular with Australians is that he
unashamedly uses a thick Australian accent, while most other
Australian television performers try to sound British or American.
"I just acted natural," Hogan said, "and everybody identified with
me." Can you imagine how bad it would be if Dolly Parton tried to
sound like Jane Fonda or Lily Tomlin?

"Four Generations Are Buried Right Here," Granddad Rankin
would whisper vigorously. Each year he pointed his cane to the
little graveyard behind Mt. Horeb Presbyterian Church in Dumplin
Valley, Jefferson County. It was always clipped clean on reunion

Sunday. Like every mountain graveyard it faces East, because the Bible teaches that Jesus will come again from the East, and no mountain family wants its loved ones facing the wrong way when Jesus comes.

Granddad whispered because cancer had stolen his voice box in 1946. Sometimes during hymn singing he whistled the tunes, especially because this annoyed my great aunts.

"I am the fifth, your mother standing here is the sixth, you are the seventh, and your children will be the eighth generation. No one," he would solemnly pronounce, "except the Cherokees, can go back further than that in East Tennessee."

At six feet four inches, Granddad was imposing, not the kind of fellow to argue with. I was convinced he founded the Rankin reunion in order to teach me that I was a seventh generation, Scotch-Irish Presbyterian East Tennessean and proud of it. Even when he told me that Thomas Rankin, who came to Dumplin Valley in *1783*, was a Republican, I didn't argue with him!

Why I Don't Chew. Deep in the secrecy of a cave near Greenback, these explorers tasted for the first time the pleasures of Red Man tobacco. When we crawled out from the fifty-six degree cave darkness into the July sun, the change in temperature plus the novelty of a First Chaw made me so red-faced and pukey sick that I have never wanted to chew again.

Tennessee boys and girls get an early start in the outdoors. We spent almost every weekend in the mountains, thanks to good scoutmasters and to having the Great Smoky Mountains fifteen miles away.

I'm second from the left on the back row.

"Some of Us Spent a Lot of Time Getting Out of Houses Like That," was my dad's first opinion of our log cabin.

The logs came from a barn near Jonesboro. John Rice Irwin said it must have been built about 1800 since an ax made the hard cuts on the ends of the big logs. (After 1800 in Upper East Tennessee, they used saws.)

Honey and I stole time during the 1982 reelection campaign to plan our new home. The October morning we first saw the barn we were so excited we were late for a campaign breakfast in Rogersville. Even after voting on election day, we stopped by McMinnville to visit "My Grandfather's House," owned by a Texas couple retiring to Tennessee to live in their ancestral home. We began to appreciate how dark and cramped log houses really were, with their puncheon floors and bare dirt yards (so you could see the snakes better), and we understood better, too, why so many Tennesseans carved GTT—Gone to Texas—on their cabin doors and went west looking for the promised land.

Delmar Caylor marked and hauled the logs 120 miles to Blackberry Farm in Miller's Cove. With the help of craftsmen from Blount and Sevier counties, Delmar and his brothers turned the old barn into a home. We saved everything we could: the hay rack became an upstairs railing; the old barn doors are the house doors today. Some old things are new. The split rail fence is from cedars we bought from John Rice Irwin. (It's not the best thing for keeping cows out of the front yard today, just as it didn't do much to keep the buffaloes out two hundred years ago.) The rock walls and chimneys are made from flat limestones that seem to sprout every spring in the fields of Dry Valley. The bluebird houses—with five eggs the spring of 1986—are part of the Bluebird Homecoming Trail to help restore the bluebird population in Tennessee.

The house faces the sunset toward the Chilhowee Mountains— "enemy mountains" when the Cherokees and Sam Houston lived there. The backyard is the Great Smokies.

While Delmar built, Dad took pictures, made suggestions, and visited with the workmen. Then we built a second cabin, this one taken from Warren County, by Hesse Creek. On a March Sunday afternoon in 1984, Dad helped us fence the front yard with white oak pickets, even though the chill and his weak heart made him uncomfortable. This cabin by the stream is officially our guest house and often my workplace. But the truth is that Honey, being from Texas, preferred the hillside open spaces where the log barn now is, and I, being an East Tennessean, couldn't imagine not having a log cabin close by a mountain creek. So we have both.

Dad died that May. He had nearly finished pasting into a scrapbook his best pictures of our cabins going up. Mother saved it for me. It's always in my study at the Governor's Residence to look at when we are not at the cabin.

How the Idea for Tennessee Homecoming '86 Grew

"How about a 'Year of the Tennessean,' to celebrate ourselves?" That was Charlotte Davidson's suggestion to Commissioner of Tourism Irving Waugh in 1980. Irving, who invented Opryland and Fan Fair, knows a good idea when he sees one, so he presented it to me. For nearly two years the idea stayed on the shelf, mostly because we were still learning what works best in government.

In the meantime Conservation Commissioner Charlie Howell said we should begin planning now for Tennessee's two-hundredth birthday in 1996. I met Alex Haley, read *Roots* for the first time, and realized more and more that people—or communities—who don't know who they are or where they come from often have a poor self-image and that people with a poor self-image rarely set high goals for themselves. Every day I saw evidence that communities—not governors—fix schools, prepare for new jobs, clean themselves up, and decide whether they will be nice places to live or not. Most of the good that is going to happen to Memphis and Maryville will be decided in Memphis and Maryville.

By 1982 all of these ideas had swirled into a thirteen-year project looking ahead to Tennessee's bicentennial, "Vision '96." It would be look-at-your-roots and plan-a-project for 1996. The focus would be on research and preservation. In December Doug Bailey suggested that my second inaugural speech in January 1983 kick off the state's bicentennial plans for the 1996 celebration. We were all excited about the success of Community Days during the 1982 campaign where, on forty-five occasions, Honey and I had worked in communities on self-help projects ranging from new libraries to nursing homes. Doug used the word *homecoming* to describe all of those people coming to Tennessee, either for the first time or returning home, because of the "simplicity and honest lifestyle" to be found here.

Since most people live from day to day or week to week and only a few historians and futurists want to look ahead thirteen years to a bicentennial, we moved the target date for our celebration ahead ten years to 1986. My second inaugural address outlined four steps for the celebrations: 1983, look at your roots and define what's special; 1984, design a community homecoming project; 1985, build that project; and "the 1986 step is for all of us to celebrate by inviting all America to come see what we've done—to come see the traditions and values of Tennessee and the wonderful differences in the three thousand places we proudly call home, to come to an American Homecoming, to Tennessee '86."

That became the program. New York and Los Angeles advertising agencies employed by some of Tennessee's largest companies began to ask for appointments with us. They were astonished by the power of the idea. During those meetings I realized that there

was one more word that by itself conveyed to most people the feelings of our celebration, so it finally became:

"*Tennessee* Homecoming '86."

It was already 1984, and still we had not figured out a logo for Tennessee Homecoming '86. Hank Dye suggested a quilted Tennessee flag. The quilt was a great symbol, but the flag didn't do much for me. Hank is the state's number one advocate of the Tennessee flag and he insisted.

"We need something warmer, homier," I said. "Drop it over a fence. Tack it on a barn. Put it in a chair."

The quilted flag came back draped over a picnic basket. It was still a little too up-town for me.

"Try a rocking chair," I suggested. Hank returned with the flag spread over the chair. I suggested we show more of the chair. What came back was a perfect and beautiful drawing. It will be a proud Tennessee symbol for years to come.

"Honey One" and "Honey Two" —that's what Peter Jenkins called his wife Barbara and Honey on our hike.

I Can Still Remember the Turn in the Trail Where Peter Jenkins Started Talking about His Idea for a Homecoming Calendar. Peter, his wife, Barbara, Honey, Drew and I had just spent thirty minutes flat on our backs resting in the November morning sun. We were in the second day of our hike along the same mountain ridges the first settlers had followed on their way to Cades Cove during the 1830's, and I understood better why it was easier for them to bump up and down the creeks than to cut their way through the rhododendron thickets. This was our way to celebrate the beginning of the fiftieth anniversary of the Great Smoky Mountains National Park.

We ended our trip early the next day, Sunday, hiking to Cades Cove in a cold, soaking rain. The descendants of settlers' families had been waiting for nearly an hour when we arrived. The caravan of old wagons, impatient horses, and drenched walkers moved across the grassy meadows of the cove. (In the excitement a television cameraman fell into the creek, some of the horses that had been with us for three days ran away, and the park superintendent fell off his mount and broke two ribs.)

The Cades Cove Primitive Baptist Church, established in 1827, was dry but there was no light and no heat. After a while the strong voices of the shaped-note singers from Wear's Valley and the primitive preaching lifted our spirits, and the warming bodies sent steam toward the church rafters. The sounds of horses and wagons driving up, clip-a-clop, outside the church added to the wonder of what it must have been like 150 years ago.

There are many Tennesseans more like the Jenkinses, who *chose* to live here, than like the Alexanders, who have been here for seven generations. Sometimes these newcomers are more interested in helping to preserve our heritage than the old-timers. It is one of the main reasons these families—and car companies—are coming to Tennessee. And they don't take it for granted.

John Rice and Elizabeth Irwin

The Fly-minder Is My Favorite Contraption at John Rice Irwin's Museum of Appalachia. At lunch, mountain women once used newspapers to shoo away flies while the men ate. The fly-minder was an invention for the mountain man who had no wife, who had a reluctant wife, or who just preferred to dine alone. Pushing the foot pedals moved the machinery, which moved the newspapers, which shooed the flies—all of which could be done while enjoying corn bread and beans.

John Rice Irwin is the former school superintendent of Anderson County who has collected two hundred fifty thousand items from Tennessee's Appalachian heritage. His homestead museum is the most interesting place Honey and I have discovered while I've been governor.

THE TENNESSEE HOMECOMING SPECIAL

Riding a passenger train across Tennessee these days is like walking across the state through back yards: most people don't expect you; you're gone before you interrupt them much; and you see them just as they are.

That was the Tennessee Homecoming Special—five days across the state, from Bristol to Memphis, seeing Tennesseans just like they were in May 1986. Some were digging postholes, hanging overalls on an outside line, working on high rafters as we passed Union Station in Nashville. Two policemen had stopped to talk by an underpass. There were women carrying aprons so full of turnip greens that Alex Haley nearly leaped off the train in admiration.

Fifty thousand people greeted the special at its sixteen stops, and I saw old friends everywhere.

"Last time you saw her she was only eleven months old and look at her now!" a proud father in Sweetwater said, pushing an eight-year-old photograph—and his nine-year-old daughter—to the front of the crowd, making sure I saw them both. She had been a baby in 1978 when I had stopped along my walk and held her in my arms. He still carried the photograph taken then, but now her hair was long and pretty, and she had grown so tall and her stomach was so full that I could barely lift her.

"Let's get another picture," the man said. "Then we'll have one from the walk and one from the train, too."

At each stop Tennessee Ernie Ford or Lynn Anderson or Carl Perkins or the Homecoming "Bookends" belted out Tennessee music, and Alex Haley complimented each community for studying its roots. Politicians of every variety beamed.

156

There were 4,000 people in Cowan, 3,000 in Tullahoma, and 3,500 in Murfreesboro—more of all ages than you would expect at every stop—waiting patiently in line to see the insides of a real passenger train. "I've seen a lot," one eighty-two-year-old man said in Cleveland, "and this is one of the things worth seeing."

Waving is the way people talk to trains.

Whistling is the way trains talk back.

So there was plenty of conversation between the Homecoming Special—which had a good loud whistle—and the people waiting along the tracks because Tennesseans know how to wave.

It made me think of walking across the state when I waved at every car and most people waved back. I remembered thinking then, *People everywhere don't wave as much as they do in Tennessee, do they?* The people on their front porches in Miller's Cove in Blount County, for example, wave at *anything* going by. But eventually you find out that their wave is a friendly cover so they can check you out without being too obvious about it. And in Miller's Cove, as in most of Tennessee, how you wave back will have a lot to do with what they think of you.

The Homecoming Special began most of these conversations by issuing two long loud whistle blasts, then one short one, then one very long one before each highway crossing.

There were crossings every few minutes (216 between Bristol and Knoxville), and Tennesseans were waiting for the train at almost every crossing. They said hello with:

The Little Kids' Wave: All five fingers, close to the face.

The Roundtable Wave: For old folks, hand above head, half way round; for *really* old folks, half a roundtable.

The Windshield Wiper Wave: A two hander, over the head and back and forth.

The Referee's Wave: Another two hander, as in what a referee does after a touchdown.

Those of us riding on the back of the train found ways to join the conversation. For example, if we gave a semaphore wave (right arm bent, moving up and down), someone along the tracks would give one back.

But the passengers had the most fun discovering and naming the different waves. There was:

The "Real-Excited-Kids" Wave: (Will Alexander identified this one.) Jumping up and down and making a lot of noise. Excited grown-ups do it, too.

The "Back-Roads-Pick-Up-Truck" Wave: (Ed Bruce saw this first.) Given by the second finger of the right hand, which is the hand on the steering wheel—never more action than that, even though the left hand is in the lap.

The "Rodeo" Wave: (Lynn Anderson) A right hand salute at the brim of the cowboy hat and then shoot your arm out straight and up to the right.

The "Ain't-I-Cute" Wave: Hardly a wave at all, mainly a priss, by a surprised lady outside Bristol. After seeing her cotton-candy hair stacked high, Tennessee Ernie Ford hollered, "Lord, you've done your hair!" as the train rolled past her back yard.

The "Ethnic" Wave: Described by Alex Haley, "Black folks were doing it. It begins with a little toss of the hand, half-hearted. Then they see A. Z. [Howard, another black man] or me, and the little toss turns into a big wave; and there is a smile and it all says, 'Hey, we're on there! It's for us, too!'"

Some of the waves spoke more loudly than any words:

"I Never-Should-Have" Waved: By the TV cameraman on the tracks above the train who got so excited when the train came he waved instead of shooting pictures, and then the train was gone.

"I-Saw-It-Before-You-Saw-It" Wave: One arm thrown straight ahead, nearly out of the socket.

"Blow-The-Whistle" Wave: A big imaginary pull with one arm, the same wave kids give from back seats of cars to truck drivers.

"Not-Me-Buddy-I'm-Too-Tough-To-Get-Carried-Away-By-An-Old-Train-But-Hello-Anyway" Wave: The last guy in a row of men to wave. This is macho stuff. Many times it's a contest to see who can show the least enthusiasm.

I'll never forget that train, especially being with my son Will, age seven, who rode the train all five days, sporting an oversized engineer's cap and bandana and holding on—most of the time—to my pants pocket with one finger.

On the first day Will pulled the emergency cord (it was supposed to be the whistle!) and stopped the train. He was scared and embarrassed. But the third day he felt pretty big thinking about it. Being with Will reminded me of climbing into the cab of a steam locomotive when *I* was his age, and my grandfather was an engineer. Riding the Homecoming Special I wondered if there could be anything more satisfying than standing at the back of a slow moving train with your seven-year-old son.

I will remember best the faces of Tennesseans. I couldn't meet the people behind the faces the same way I did when I had six months to walk across the state. But I could tell a lot about Tennessee by looking at those faces—secretaries waving flags from office buildings, fathers hugging daughters, veterans wearing legion hats, older couples topping berries on back porches, grandparents holding grandchildren high to see the train, and everyone's eyes glistening when "God Bless the U.S.A." climaxed the musical show at each stop.

The faces I saw showed me that Tennesseans believe in themselves and in the three thousand places with names they proudly call home. The spirit and the pride I saw are greater now than when I walked across Tennessee eight years ago. As this growing spirit and pride shapes the state's future, Tennessee Homecoming '86 will have served as a beginning, and the Homecoming Special can be a symbol of our future as well as a reminder of the past.

Acknowledgments

The photographs presented in this scrapbook have been selected from among the thousands that have come my way. Some we purchased from the state's Division of Photographic Services; others came from newspapers; many were snapshots or photographs taken by Honey or me or by friends from all over Tennessee who kindly sent them along for us to enjoy. We have tried hard to identify and thank every photographer. To anyone we missed, I apologize. To everyone who contributed, "Thanks."

Don Foster/*Nashville Banner* (p. 2); Bill Welch (p. 6); Robin Hood/*Chattanooga News-Free Press* (p. 8, p. 10, p. 114); Bill Gibson/ *Daily Times* (p. 12); *Independent-Appeal* (Selmer) (p. 18); Gerald Holly/*Tennessean* (p. 27); Mike O'Neal/*Chattanooga News-Free Press*, 1979 (p. 27, p. 28); Dan Loftin/*Tennessean* (p. 28); Bill Fitz-Patrick/ the White House (p. 62); Terry Moore/*Knoxville News-Sentinel* (p. 69); William R. Wilburn/*Greenville Sun* (p. 71); Vic Cooley/*Nashville Banner* (p. 84); Tillman Crane/*Daily Times* (p. 119).

State of Tennessee, Division of Photographic Services, Photographers: Earl Warren, Jr., Robin Hood, Jed DeKalb, Murray Lee, Tillman Crane, Jim Hagans, Tom Jaynes.

Davis Adkisson; the Alexander Committee: Harry Butler and Mark Gill; Howard Baker; Nancy Jarman; Peter Jenkins; Marc Lavine; Louis Lockhart; Nissan Motor Manufacturing Corp., USA; John Parish; Jan Talley; Tennessee Film, Tape, and Music Commission; Cyndy B. Waters; and Eddie Williams. A special thanks to cartoonists Sandy Campbell, *Tennessean*; Richard Crowson, *Jackson Sun*; and Charlie Daniel, *Knoxville Journal*.